The ASSIGNMENT

DEVON BLANTON

Dedication

This book is dedicated to the obscure, unseen quiet servants who are my heroes. They have somehow discovered the secret of life. I honor them for their steady hand of faithfulness and determination to serve relentlessly through every storm. God sees and God rewards. The first shall be last and the last shall be first.

I also dedicate this book to my precious wife, Jill who has stood by my side through innumerable assignments and has radically improved my life beyond words. She is my joy and my life-mate.

I include my children, Evan and Eric. Joyfully I get to add our daughter, Logan via marriage to Eric along with our sweet granddaughter London. I am so blessed that each of you are in my life. I love you forever and always.

To my Executive Assistant Tina Owen, who has worked tirelessly to further the Kingdom of God without the first complaint even on her days off. She has stood faithfully for Jesus and has affected many lives for which I am most grateful. Thank you for your humble service to our King.

Keys for Unlocking These Pages

The numbered line of each page is for quick reference. The end of the chapter has information that refers to the specific page and line for instant access to the **main point** of each paragraph. Take note of the emphasis provided, e.g. words in **bold**, *italics,* <u>underlined</u> and referenced Scriptures. All these have emphasis for a specific purpose and are meaningful to the point of the lesson. Also provided is a "Key Study Words in Context" section for the reader. Be sure to study these words (bold/italics) and learn their meanings. It is easy to overlook key words as we read assuming we know the meanings. There is a point to these words and a reason for their selection. Every reader will benefit from understanding each of these. This study is based upon the foundational precepts of God's Word. Carefully explore every concept presented as it may change lives and bolster the Kingdom of God. This is the purpose of this study.

Chapters

Preface...5

1. The Deepest Craving – Significance.......................7

2. The Mirror...16

3. The Plan 25

4. Vulnerability 42

5. Learning the Art of Enduring Well....................51

6. The Inability to Cope 66

7. Superstition (More Tricks)................................77

8. The Pursuing 88

9. Divine Persuasion 105

10. Entanglement 112

11. The Assignment of Loss 119

12. It's Right in Front of You 125

13. For the Win! 133

Preface

Before you turn a page, take a moment to stop, breathe and ask the Lord to speak His truths to you aloud, clearly and concisely. It is my prayer that He has anointed these writings not as the Holy Writ but as something that boldly screams the provocative and compelling truths that intentionally exist within those blessed pages.

Perhaps one of the most puzzling questions for modern society is "why am I here?" The approach of The ASSIGNMENT is that if we understand the assignment, then the rest is easy. By the end of this book, you will know the reason for your assignment and its primary purposes. This discovery can be exhilarating and quite liberating. It addresses why we are here, what is our specific purpose and why do bad things happen to good people? These questions seem to stifle the modern believer and often leave them feeling confused. The concepts displayed within these pages are biblically plausible and easily harmonize with its premise.

Over many years the Americanized Christian Church developed philosophies and mechanisms in order to protect that particular perspective. However when we step back into the contextual biblical world as it was written, we can often see its true meaning more clearly. *The Assignment* does not contend that there is a new doctrine or some departure from the fundamentals of our faith. Rather, it reiterates them but from a revelational perspective.

There is a certain joy in discovery. Even small questions can trip us up and leave us feeling incomplete. The discoveries in the following pages could mean a life change and a literal game changer for its reader. Patiently glean through the thought processes that are presented here. I think it will move you and ultimately bless you.

There is no reason to write a theologically influenced book apart from its purpose to advance the Kingdom of God. If this is its end result, it will have been worth every moment of prayer, fasting and the pain of the total birthing process. My prayer is that it feeds the core of the soul at its deepest level and resets the game plan for success and victory for the Cross of Christ.

In my usual writing style, I have tried to lovingly and yet clearly express biblical truths with boldness and fervor. Sometimes funny and sometimes cutting, the truth shines through as though the clouds open up and a beam of light becomes blatantly obvious. We have too long hidden behind our culture and the Gospel has suffered because of it. It is my earnest prayer that within these pages, clarity and a distinct understanding of our assignment becomes plain and easy for us all. Ponder carefully the biblically sound mechanisms of faith support found in these discoveries. Our day has come but we will never approach our assignment until we know what it is. Once we truly get this we will be world changers and we will begin our trek to the eminent return of Christ. These discoveries have changed my life and I pray that they do the same for you!

Chapter 1
The Deepest Craving – Significance

Never in the history of time has the human experience demanded an answer to the question, "Why am I here?" more than it does today. The American ideal has shifted from working the fields and factories to working with digits in the cyber world of illusion. At least, when we worked a field or built something in a factory there was tangible evidence that something had truly changed. Even cash money is less noticeable in banks as entire financial empires exist without the first exchange of the Federal Reserve Notes that we have historically called "cash." Living in a world where seemingly nothing is real can leave us with a powerful need for significance and meaning. Even our communication method reduces us to the quick push of a few buttons. We no longer need to be "smart" because our smart phones do that for us.

Since our world has insisted on being *modern*, we have lost our footing and consequently struggle to feel connected to anything. There seems to be little difference between the believer and the typical lost soul who wanders and meanders through life merely sleeping, eating and working. We all have more than enough to do and yet the days and the years seem shorter than ever before. The speed at which time blows by us is like a fast plane and blatantly obvious. This is true not only to the elderly but also quite shockingly to the young as well. It feels as though we have been plunged into some kind of black hole where time rushes into a vortex faster and faster as we approach the apparent end of it all. We can't stop it. No matter what we do, time continues to speed by and no human on earth can alter it. If you have a young child at home right now, go ahead and put your seat belt on. Before you know it, you will be paying for

1 college, wondering what in the world happened to the
2 previous fleeting years. Your spirit may feel as though you
3 are still twenty-five years of age but your mirror
4 **unabashedly** tells another story. This is all the more reason
5 to be deliberate about the things we *must* do and focus on
6 living life more fully.
7
8   The passing of time and other experiences in life can
9 leave us feeling empty and unfulfilled. Some tend to believe
10 that making more money is the solution but it won't fix this
11 and conversely, making a vow of poverty cannot fix it either.
12 We basically work to secure our lifestyles in a manner that
13 is socially acceptable, depending on what we think of as
14 normal. Nevertheless at the end of the day, even if we acquire
15 financial security, we still do not necessarily feel that we
16 have found our reason to be. Though many have tried to use
17 money as the measure of success and therefore significance,
18 it can never really do the job. It merely makes us feel *a*
19 *momentary sense of accomplishment and we can often*
20 *misinterpret that as significance*. However once the thrill of
21 the money is gone, there often abides an empty and
22 unfulfilled spirit deep within the individual. Sadly due to the
23 spiritual immaturity of the average modern Christian, they
24 don't appear to fare any better than the lost. That is a very
25 sad commentary for the church because she can do much
26 better.
27
28   All this can leave us in a **quandary** about life. This
29 unaddressed deep abiding need for fulfillment quietly
30 mourns in the background of all that we do. Even the best
31 love relationship can feel the brunt of it once everything is
32 said and done. When the initial thrill is gone, many move on
33 to more exciting pursuits. It seems that they have become
34 addicted to the chase rather than having an inner peace that
35 comes from true contentment. The **carnal** trappings of this
36 world do not easily move those who find real contentment.

1   They see goods and modern conveniences as mere tools for
2   the trip rather than assuming they are the destination. It is
3   true, that owning **things** must not become the destination.
4   Simply having the knowledge of this is not enough. It is
5   unlikely that the answer for the looming question of our
6   significance is found merely by denying things of this world
7   the right to *own us*. There is more to it. *We* must be the boss
8   of things and not allow things to be the boss of us. In truth
9   most people never really get this. It is a game-changer to
10   arrive at this understanding but it is not the final answer to
11   our much deeper inner quest to know more fully why we are
12   here. By connecting with the God who made us, we find that
13   there is something much deeper and something much more
14   personal that speaks to our inner being. Only He truly knows
15   what our purpose is. Yes, it's easy to assume that because we
16   have a certain skill, that this somehow is the end-all solution
17   to our dilemma. The fact is we cannot find our truest
18   meaning until we connect with the one who originally
19   authored it. Initially only God can see the end result. He
20   knows why He wants us to do a certain thing. **Cooperating**
21   with Him is the best method to finding it. After all, we cannot
22   assume that coercing God into doing things our way would
23   result in a favorable response. If we think we can force Him
24   then we do not know His true nature. He is not our puppet or
25   our butler. He is God Almighty. We submit to Him, not the
26   other way around.
27
28   We must establish the fact that God is **not all about**
29   **us** as many presume. Oh yes, He loves us beyond compare
30   but there is something that drives Him far more than *our*
31   needs. **His purposes** are the driving forces that greatly
32   outrank our often superficial perceptions of need or want. He
33   is determined to accomplish that which He foreordained. Be
34   assured that He loved us so very much that He sent His
35   "ONLY" Son so that we could have life and be with Him
36   forever. There is no doubt about that. However, if we think

1   the creation of the world is for the purpose of pampering us,
2   we are sorely mistaken. The complete picture of life as we
3   know it is not supposed to be about us; it's about Him. The
4   flowers, trees, rivers, animals, oceans and mountains may be
5   beautiful to us and a blessing for us to enjoy but the entire
6   scene is about Him and His Glory. We have been duped into
7   thinking that God exists solely for us. To believe that is an
8   error in judgement concerning His nature, His majesty and
9   the expanse of His domain. We must fully grasp that
10   everything exists for His sake and His Glory INCLUDING
11   US. Could this be why we struggle so much with
12   understanding our significance? Are we so *narcissistic* that
13   we cannot see that it is supposed to be about Him and not
14   us? We have such an ego-centric perspective that it *skews*
15   our perceptions, blinding us to the truth concerning our true
16   reason to be. His purposes are not about us amassing great
17   wealth although He taught us how to save money and to be
18   necessarily frugal. We presume that because Jesus came to
19   the earth to save us that the entire universe and all of creation
20   was for us alone. That reveals our introspective arrogance
21   and our lack of understanding of His true purposes. Through
22   this ongoing creation process, revealing God's glory was
23   always paramount. Once we gain that understanding, we can
24   know that we are a *part* of that plan and that we are not the
25   exclusive purpose for it. Granted, He sees us as a *very*
26   *significant* part of that plan but we must *always* remember
27   that the whole of the plan as I have already stated, is not
28   about us. We are not the focal point here; He is. We are the
29   recipients of His mercy and grace. In light of this, we should
30   be deeply humbled that He included us and promised us
31   joint-heirship with Christ. Oh my, what an unthinkable gift!
32
33   Let's go a step further. This *erroneous* "all about me"
34   attitude has *permeated* an already narcissistic religious
35   world and it has flung us wildly into the riptide of greed and
36   insignificance. The cost of this errant behavior is staggering

1   to us as individuals, the Church and to the ***Kingdom of God***.
2   First let's establish that God doesn't "need" us. He doesn't
3   need anything or anybody. The Gift of God is simply that, a
4   gift. We don't deserve it. Our problem is that we often say
5   that we don't and then turn around and not only do we expect
6   it; we demand it. We forget that God is so powerful that with
7   a flick of His little finger, He could wipe us all from
8   existence and eliminate us from His memory as though we
9   had never been. What's more, if He were to do that, He
10 would be fully justified because it is ALL a gift and a
11 privilege to be born with such an amazing opportunity to
12 bow at His feet. If we see this in any other way than that of
13 a gift, we essentially are the problem. How can we feel
14 "significance" if we are nothing more than spoiled brats who
15 demand that we be treated as if the whole world revolves
16 around us? We have the wrong concept of why we are here
17 and more than that, we have the wrong concept of who God
18 is. Let's all get this in our heads; God is not needy. To know
19 Him is both an honor and a privilege, not a right. As a result
20 of our distorted view of God, we spend a lifetime spinning
21 our wheels and getting nowhere. We are not the center of the
22 universe but out of the bowels of mercy, God gave us the
23 privilege of knowing Him personally through our born-again
24 kinship with His Son, Jesus.
25
26   Sometimes addiction can get in the way of our ability
27 to prefer the truly good things in life. If we are addicted to
28 ourselves, how can we have an appetite for more needed
29 things? It's like going to the candy store just before supper
30 time. We cannot possibly enjoy the things that are necessary
31 for our well-being if we fill up on candy. If we believe that
32 *things* are the destination, then we will fill up on those while
33 starving ourselves of the things that would build and
34 strengthen us. It's not really hard to understand. We prefer
35 the desserts over the veggies. Children will sometime fight
36 preferring the sweets. They don't want the peas and carrots.

They want what ***they*** *want*! Of course, if they got their way, it would eventually kill them and ruin their hope for a future. I contend that this is what we have done in our society today. Essentially we have believed that the world is about us when in fact, it is about the will of God. Even Jesus refused to do His own will by totally submitting to His Father's wishes. He did nothing for Himself and He refused to pursue His needs above the desires of the Father. This is a great lesson for us today. It is no wonder that we struggle with significance. We are a people who are generally out of balance and we are presumptuous concerning our role in this privilege we call space and time. Our ***mandate*** from the Lord is to build the Kingdom of God. He says not to worry about what we will eat or what clothes we will wear. Seeking first the Kingdom of God and being in right standing with Him is required before all these other things will come. If we prefer *things* above the Kingdom, we are out of order, "But seek ye first the kingdom of God, and his righteousness; and all these things shall be added unto you". Matthew 6:33.

God formed our spirits and sent us into these bodies - these jars of clay by way of Adam so that we could fulfill ***His*** will, not our own. This is our true assignment and in this alone can we find our significance in life. Many have tried everything they can think of to reach this lofty goal of inner peace and significance. Unless they conclude that God is the center, all their efforts will end in vain. We cannot be the center if God holds that post.

Chapter 1
The Deepest Craving - Significance

Key Word Studies in Context

Craving – (Pg. 7, #2) A great desire or yearning for something specific. Usually is the result of an extreme need or desire.

Significance – (Pg. 7, #2) to believe, feel or acquire a true meaning or purpose; to feel self-value.

Unabashedly – (Pg. 8, #4) not ashamed or apologetic.

Quandary – (Pg. 8, #28), a dilemma, state of perplexity or confusion.

Carnal – (Pg. 8, #35) Fleshly, from a human perspective; devoid of godly perspective.

Narcissistic) – (Pg. 10, #12), ego-centric, self-centered, all about one's self lifestyle or point of view.

Skew – (Pg. 10, #14), to see something outside of its original intended meaning, a wrong view.

Erroneous – (Pg. 10, #33), something that is errant or incorrect.

Permeate – (Pg. 10, #34), to penetrate, pervade or saturate.

Kingdom of God – (Pg. 11, #1), this is the establishment of the will of God on earth as it is in Heaven.

Mandate – (Pg. 12, #12), to require, demand or requirement.

Workbook Activities

1. Before you go further in this study, write what you think your purpose is in the space provided below.

2. List some things that rob us of our daily focus. (Pg. 7, #4-18)

3. Discuss why time quickly passing by is a factor as to how we should live. (Pg. 7, #20-35; Pg. 8, #1-6)

4. We often feel a sense of accomplishment when we obtain things. Is that temporary or is it a permanent sense of significance? (Pg. 8, #8-26)

5. Explain why "having things" must not become the destination. (Pg. 8, #28-36; Pg. 9, #1-26)

6. Discuss why the central focus of the plan of God is on Him and not on us. (Pg. 9, #28-36; Pg. 10, #1-31)

7. What does it mean when we say, "God doesn't need us?" (Pg. 10, #33-36; Pg. 11, #1-24)?

8. Explain the following: "We cannot possibly enjoy the things that are necessary for our well-being if we fill up on candy." (Pg. 11, #26-36; Pg. 12, #1-19).

9. Discuss the primary purpose for us to be alive? (Pg. 12, #21-28)

Chapter 2
The Mirror

Perhaps the hardest thing we do is to look closely into our own emotional mirrors. We don't like seeing the flaws that lurk under the surface. They hide there like dirt under a rug. Sooner or later they will rear their ugly heads and expose us. Each of these flaws has a distinct voice. They constantly remind us that failure is expected and emotional pain is normal. Of course these are all carefully laid snares intended to undermine our hope to ever be free. This kind of freedom *eludes* most westernized human beings that are desperate to know true peace. Let me further explain. If we are indebted to someone, we are never truly free until that debt is settled. The same holds true with our emotional debts based upon the negative voices that constantly sing their chants day after day and night after night. We should never ignore these debts no matter if they are there inadvertently or by evil intention. It is imperative to pay these debts in full if we intend to live in peace. That begs the question; how can we accomplish shutting down those negative voices that wreak a lifetime of havoc on our emotions? We must address them directly and fix them at the root in order to stop them and settle it once and for all.

To begin, let's discover how these voices get there in the first place. They usually occur during the times when we are most emotionally vulnerable. Sometimes our parents don't know when these *imprints* occur because they don't live in our brains. They can't possibly know every moment that we need reassuring or affirming. Certainly every parent should know that when their child plays a sport or an instrument, to offer them encouragement during those times but what about those quiet secret moments of self-doubt? If a child doesn't have the proper tools to sustain against such negative thought processes, he or she can easily fall prey to it and believe it to be ***normal***. Because of this ***pernicious*** ploy and natural vulnerability, we are easy to program to fail without realizing it. Do we think that this is God's way? It seems that few address such horrific mental thinking processes that in the end maim and ultimately destroy our hope of success. We simply accept them as normal. They're not. They are snares that entangle and create emotional strongholds. Here are some ways to combat this experience so that we can get on with our assignments in life.

- Identify God's ***sovereignty*** as the thing that matters most.
- Accept that we must change our thinking to God's thinking. *We* have to do it.
- Build better memories and forget negative things that are in the past. In other words, don't give credibility to those things that haunt us from years ago. *"Brethren, I count not myself to have apprehended: but this one thing I do, forgetting those things which are behind, and reaching forth unto those things which are before." (Philippians 3:13).*
- Here's another one. It sounds simple but it's very powerful: *"Finally, brethren, whatsoever things are true, whatsoever things are honest, whatsoever things are just, whatsoever things are pure, whatsoever things are lovely, whatsoever things are of good report; if there be any virtue, and if there be any praise, think on these things". (Philippians 4:8).*
- Be the boss of your own brain and tell it what to do and how to think. Think deliberately rather than by default! We do this best by submitting to God's thinking.
- Forgive everyone including you and move on. Don't hang out at the emotional city dump! Get out of there!

- View past memories from an adult perspective rather than seeing it from the eyes of a wounded child.
- Absolutely refuse to accept any negative voice from the past or the present. Remember that constructive criticism is not the same as a negative voice. Constructive means to build up.
- Stop hanging around people who constantly drain you emotionally. They are using you as a pity comforter. Stop it. You can still love them but you must move on. We cannot carry everyone else's burdens. That's not our assignment. Even if you are a counselor, you must not take their pain home with you. That doesn't help anyone.

Successful self-examination is nearly impossible to accomplish by some because they have spent years working on how to overlook their flaws. They simply believe that they are that way because of their lot in life. They often say things such as, "That's just the way I'm made" as though it's a DNA issue. What they really mean is that because it takes some considerable pain and lots of work to make that transition, they are unwilling to do it. After all, when you pick at an old wound, it just makes it sore again. Accepting that there may be something negative about us further complicates our emotions and perpetuates the agony. If we accept our personalities as they are, even though we don't like them, then we have a built-in self-disdain. This complicates things further. Living within a physical frame that has a broken emotional base often means we don't respect ourselves and makes for a very unhappy life. Oddly enough, this happens far too often without the first effort to resist only because we believe this is normal. It is sad but true.

Until we muster enough courage to do something about the one in the mirror, we are destined to live a life

1   that's little more than rock-bottom survival. Living that way
2   negates inner peace which is the most sought after desire in
3   life. The first step in changing our lives is to recognize that
4   there is a need for a change. We can't respond to our own
5   needs if we refuse to acknowledge that they exist.
6
7   Sometimes people with self-esteem issues
8   overcompensate by becoming braggarts and self-absorbed.
9   In such cases, peers can reject them simply because they are
10   obnoxious rather than for the root of their problem, whatever
11   that might be. Actually, this kind of ***bombastic*** behavior is
12   often nothing more than an attempt to convince others as
13   well as one's own self that they are normal hoping to be
14   accepted. They tend to believe that these odd perspectives
15   are simply ***eccentric*** rather than weird and unacceptable.
16   What's more, they often spend a lifetime feeling anger
17   toward those who refuse to agree with their personal
18   assessment. The process can be complex. In some cases, this
19   broken behavior causes out-right rejection from their peers,
20   further worsening their already abysmal self-image. The
21   result is that it compounds and then recycles itself. In other
22   words, as they fight to hide their pain by pretending it's not
23   there, they spend a lifetime convincing others to agree with
24   them. When others do not agree with their errant personal
25   assessment, it deepens their self-disdain and further
26   complicates their emotional state. The process can repeat
27   itself over and over until it becomes completely unbearable
28   and ultimately emotionally paralyzing. At this point, some
29   turn to coping mechanisms such as prescription or illicit
30   drugs off the street in order to survive life. It's not supposed
31   to be that way. We have the inborn skills to cope and change
32   but if we spend a lifetime covering or ignoring them, it can
33   take a lot of difficult and uncomfortable emotional work to
34   dig those skills back out. In fact, these skills are often so
35   deeply buried that they can be totally forgotten. When this
36   happens, many people find themselves in a constant

1 emotional malaise, doomed to remain there for the rest of
2 their lives because they cannot access their coping skills.
3 They feel powerless to deal with common issues of life. This
4 is how people lose their zest for life. If we believe that our
5 world cannot improve, then we are bound to remain in our
6 emotional mess. Nothing could be further from the truth but
7 if we *believe* we can't, then we won't. When this occurs, our
8 assignments are pushed to the side. Life becomes too big and
9 the assignment becomes the least of our worries. We remain
10 in a constant state of personal emergency so much so that the
11 very idea of having an assignment is overwhelming. ***Life's***
12 ***circumstances become the boss*** and dictate that which we
13 will and will not do. We then feel there is no room for more
14 stress by adding what God wants us to do. These negative
15 circumstances become so powerful in our minds that they
16 force our belief system to concur with them and that in turn
17 puts the brakes on any hope for change. Do you see how it
18 works? Bad thinking rises and rules like a mad dog. It so
19 dominates and forces compliance that we give in to its
20 demands. It is so sickening to our spirit that we become
21 emotionally incapacitated. It's a clever ploy, isn't it? Few
22 have the wherewithal to stand up and deny its presumption
23 to rule. They have so bought into the lie of the negative voice
24 that they eventually don't even try to resist. As such, they
25 spend a lifetime living with a domineering, bossy, rude and
26 arrogant dictator, called "self." It's not just "self" that's the
27 problem, it's a *sick* "self" and sometimes we just need to get
28 help.
29
30   Leaving a broken emotional state unattended will
31 only worsen in time. When we reject the idea of fixing the
32 actual root of the problem, the self-hate continues to deepen
33 until the individual finds himself in extreme depression
34 and/or complete social isolation. Yes, the mirror can be a
35 painful experience but conversely the journey can also be
36 successful. It takes a lot of work. A good counselor knows

1 how to negotiate this journey and I strongly recommend
2 them. Most people lack the skill or the will to accomplish
3 this bold trek. We can see this by recognizing the condition
4 they are in and realizing that they have likely been there for
5 a long period of time. Get help from someone who knows
6 the depth and pain of this dilemma. It will change your whole
7 world and make life fun and worth living! The key to start
8 with is believing it doesn't have to stay this way.
9
10   Why would Satan go to these lengths to create such
11 a devastating environment for the believer? His efforts are a
12 sure way to keep people from doing what Jesus spoke of
13 most often and that is, operating the Kingdom. If we are
14 overwhelmed with our own painful world then we become
15 incapacitated and can't do anything else. Our assignment
16 goes unattended while we nurse our pain for a potential
17 lifetime. We *can* fix and heal the broken person in the mirror.
18 Thankfully Jesus is in the healing business. He can satisfy
19 the soul. He can mend a broken heart and put us back in the
20 game. His plan is for us to operate the Kingdom of God every
21 day. We must stand up and refuse to be pawns of the enemy
22 by yielding our hearts AND minds to Christ. If our struggle
23 is too great then by all means, get some help from a pastor
24 or a good Christian counselor. At this point, our main goal
25 should be to be set free so that we can taste life in its fullest
26 and complete our mission here on earth. This world is not
27 our home. We are aliens and strangers sent on a mission to
28 change the world.

The Mirror
Chapter 2

Key Word Studies in Context

<u>Elude</u> – (Pg. 16, #12), to deliberately avoid or escape something.

<u>Imprint</u> – (Pg. 16, #29), an accepted deeply rooted experience considered to be the standard by which one would live and think. This is what establishes an individual's "normal."

<u>Normal</u> – (Pg. 17, #2), a subjective point of view of things no longer believed to be unusual. God establishes the true "normal." Humans attempt to normalize things to their own advantage. That is a critically flawed perspective of truth. God is the ultimate establisher of the real "normal."

<u>Pernicious</u> – (Pg. 17, #2), intentionally devious, evil, of no good purpose, sneaky and with no regard for causing pain to others.

<u>Sovereignty</u> – (Pg. 17, #12), extreme power or control without the need for external intervention. Individually complete and needing no external assistance at any level.

<u>Bombastic</u> – (Pg. 19, #11), pompous, overblown or arrogant.

<u>Eccentric</u> – (Pg. 19, #15), not common, unusual.

Workbook Activities

1. What does it mean when we say, "each of these flaws has a distinct voice?" (Pg. 16, #4-24)

2. Discuss the validity and power of imprints, both good and bad. (Pg. 16, #26-35; Pg. 17, #1-10)

3. Discuss the tools to combat the snares of life. (Pg. 17, #12-36; Pg. 18, #1-13)

4. Successful self-examination is nearly impossible to accomplish by most people because they have spent years learning how to overlook their flaws. Discuss this in detail. (Pg. 18 #15-33)

5. We can't respond to our own needs if we refuse to see that they exist. Please explain. (Pg. 18 #35-36; Pg. 19, #1-5)

6. Often our assignments get pushed to the side. How does this happen?
(Pg. 19, #7-36; Pg. 20, #1-28)

7. Why is it necessary to fix a problem at its root?
(Pg. 20, #30-36; Pg. 21, #1-8)

8. Satan's scheme is to preoccupy until our time is done. Discuss why this is and what methods he uses to accomplish this. (Pg. 21, #10-28)

Chapter 3
The Plan

The one question that is continually asked by not only the Christian community but also by non-believers as well, is "If God is such a loving God, then why do bad things still happen in the world?" The most overlooked fact that establishes a foundational understanding about this is that the war between God and Satan is still raging. It's not over yet and we were born right in the middle of the supernatural exchange between them. Why God chose these mechanisms of time and space to wage war will remain a mystery until we live completely in the realm of the supernatural. That cannot occur until we leave these bodies.

Let's begin with a basic and simple overview of what took place in Heaven concerning the uprising of Lucifer and his *imps*.

Note: Here is an interesting *hypothesis* based on *evidentiary precept* for you to consider. Please recognize that much of what we know about this subject has been determined based on precept, hypothesis and basic logic. It is a simple matter of putting pieces of the puzzle together as we understand first the Bible and the known fundamentals of science. True science when it is rigorously put through its paces ultimately results in a *protagonistic* view of the Holy Scriptures. Read each line slowly and carefully so you won't miss anything.

- Part of Satan's original job was to worship over the throne of God. Ezekiel 28:13 says, *"You were in Eden, the garden of God. Every precious stone was your covering: The ruby, the topaz, and the diamond; the beryl, the onyx, and the jasper; the lapis lazuli, the turquoise, and the emerald; and the gold, the workmanship of your settings* (Hebrew is *tophs* which means timbrels, a musical instrument) *and sockets* (Hebrew is *neqeb* which means pipes or flutes), *was in you. On the day that you were created they were prepared."* It seems that the light of God that reflected off the jewels of Lucifer's breastplate made sounds of music, i.e., praise. The Hebrew name "Lucifer" means *light bearer*. Based on this and other information we now believe that he literally overshadowed the throne of God and the jewels on his breastplate reflected the light of God to the total realm of existence and God's creation. This light was the frequency (sound) of praise. It was an extremely glorious position. Not only could he see the light of God but he experienced its power going through him. Some people still seek that experience today. The question is, can they handle it and is it theirs to share?

- He was the apparent leader of one third of the angels in Heaven and became arrogant. (Rev. 12:4).
- Because of his ancient and lofty position, Satan was revered and admired by the angels under his direct authority.
- He became exalted and sought to set up his own kingdom above the throne of God. Isaiah 14:12-15, *"How you have fallen from heaven, O star of the morning, son of the dawn! You have been cut down to the earth. You who have weakened the nations! 13 But you said in your heart, 'I will ascend to heaven; I will raise my throne above the stars of God, and I will sit on the mount of assembly in the recesses of the north. 14 I will ascend above the heights of the clouds; I will make myself like the Most High.' 15 Nevertheless you will be thrust down to Sheol, to the recesses of the pit."*

- The Lord rebuked him and Michael the arch angel kicked him out of Heaven. We believe this based on the dominant role that Michael has in the book of Revelation as he wars against the "dragon" and his armies. We also see their confrontation as they argue over the body of Moses in Jude 9. In Luke 10:18, Jesus said, *"... I beheld Satan as lightning fall from heaven."*

- Satan was thrown down to the earth (spiritually and physically) literally into its atmosphere (Ephesians 2:2). He took a third of the angels with him leaving an empty space in Heaven.

- Let's examine the idea of the three primary angels, as we know them in the Bible. We can see that these primary angels served each respective God-head, i.e., The Father's corresponding angel was Michael (means Prince of God and also Strength of God) and Then the Holy Spirit's corresponding angel would be Gabriel (the announcer of God, His champion) then Jesus later identified as being the light of the world, His corresponding angel would was Lucifer, (meaning the son of the morning; light bearer). This may be a key indicator as to why the Son of God came to earth to redeem mankind rather than the Father or the Holy Spirit respectively. Lucifer must have been under the direct authority or *auspices* of the Son of God and therefore, Jesus came to set things right and replenish His losses with the souls of men. This appears to be the case. This is only a hypothesis based on precept.

- Satan began to exploit his kingdom on the earth. IN THEORY, the city of the kingdom of Satan is the land of "Nod." This is where Cain allegedly found his wife. Some believe that he married one of Satan's fallen angels and formed a child by the name of Enoch thus forming the *Nephilim* race. Please note that "Enoch" mentioned here is not the same as the Prophet. Many believe that God sent the world-wide flood to eliminate this fallen race. Keep in mind that this is a theory. Nevertheless Jewish tradition believes this idea to be *plausible*. Based on the *empirical* pieces of the puzzle, it seems possible. The Scripture does not state this implicitly so it remains a theory.

- It appears that since Heaven was at that point devoid of a huge number of spirits (1/3 of Heaven), Jesus came to earth, created a living soul (Adam) in order to replenish the missing angelic worshipers in Heaven. He would do so with souls of mankind through the blood of the Lamb. Jesus stated that He came for the purpose of "glorifying His Father." He taught us to worship the Father by His own example.

- Satan saw what Jesus was up to so he succeeded at corrupting Adam and his seed (Genesis 3). His apparent hope was to corrupt the seed of man so that there would be no way that man would qualify to be the "called of God" but Jesus had a plan. We believe that Satan knew that Jesus would come to reclaim the world for the Kingdom of God so he corrupted his human replacement that God had created as Adam. His plan did not succeed in the end. Christ greatly outgunned him with His salvation plan.

- Jesus knew that Satan robbed Heaven of all those angelic worshipers so for His Father's sake, Jesus came to earth which was Satan's alleged throne, scooped up dirt that Satan walked on and from that HE formed man. Right under his nose, Jesus created man and put his supernatural life-spirit in him. Later Jesus took a giant step over the DNA of man and came into the world via the womb of a virgin. Because of this, He wasn't corrupted through the fallen seed of man. The Holy Spirit supernaturally implanted the seed of God into her womb and Jesus was born. It was a slap in the face of Satan because Jesus *corrupted* his pernicious plans by creating a living soul right out of the territory of Satan. It seems that it was only *fair* since Satan took Jesus' crew right out of Heaven that Jesus set out to take it back. He would use that same *dirt* (i.e., flesh) to introduce the Savior of the world. Why does Satan hate you? Satan had robbed Heaven of its completeness and then Jesus in turn goes to the earth and makes it impossible for Satan to rise to his hopeful god-like status. At the creation of man, the race was on! Satan intended for us to be his property but God said no! Satan hates you because God apparently created us *lower life forms* (humans) to take his now abandoned position in Heaven. The reason for our creation is to "worship" the Father. Do you wonder why that element is so important? It's evidently because we replace the previous employee. Satan's attempts to foil the plan of God were met at the highest level. Jesus Himself led the charge against Satan to establish our right to be "joint heirs" with Him. Now do you see why Satan hates you so? Not only will we replace him, we will be "joint heirs" with Christ! "And if children, then heirs; heirs of God, and joint-heirs with Christ; if so be that we suffer with him, that we may be also glorified together". (Romans 8:17). That simply means that we share what's coming to Jesus in all of His Glory. We will sit with Him on His throne! Now that has to make the devil mad! Our form originated from the dirt under his feet and still God loved us and promised that we would be exalted above the position of the former worship leader! Satan had never been given permission to imagine such a high position as a joint heir. All this and more is available all because of what Jesus did for us. The only way to get there is to go through Jesus. No one else's sacrifices can even remotely compare to what Jesus did for these feeble jars of clay!

- When Jesus arrived on the scene in the New Testament, Satan tried to corrupt Him by offering Him the same kind of temptations that he had previously offered Adam (Genesis 3). He aimed his offer at the human *will*, the fleshly human side of Jesus just as he did to Adam previously in the Garden (Matthew 4:1-11). Jesus responded by reminding Satan about the rules of engagement. He quoted the Holy Scriptures.

- Jesus knew the only way to redeem fallen man was to become the pure and spotless sacrifice in their stead. He went to the cross and provided the only way for man's spirit to regenerate back to life as it was before the fall of Adam.

- Jesus then left the earth but made available to us His Holy Spirit so that we can carry on until the time comes for His eventual return.

- Fact – It's not over yet. Satan has not been bound or cast into the lake of fire. The battle still rages. The fight between good and evil is not completed. We are still in the middle of the battle. Don't forget that God wins. Our instructions from the Apostle Paul are to endure hardness as a good soldier. We are soldiers of the light, bearing His armor and as we are sent into this battle to establish His Kingdom. (2 Timothy 2:3).

- We have been born to establish God's Kingdom on this earth and to **propagate** His Glory. Satan's plan is to stop that. It is easy to see his godless works everywhere. He is evil and loves to corrupt everything he touches.

The Plan

- We are soldiers assigned to build God's Kingdom and restake His claim on the earth that He created but Satan has corrupted.
- Sin is still in the world and evil abounds. The season of God's victory is approaching but until then, bad things will happen. If we will serve Him, this world will see more of God's Glory all around us. Instead, we tend to meander through life without activating our real reason for being here; that is to serve the Lord.

Perhaps now that you have considered each of those interesting ideas, the reason why we are here is beginning to make more sense. For us to think that our spirits coupled with these human bodies are here solely to propagate the human race is very short sighted. We presume that because Christ came to earth to redeem mankind that this entire plan was solely for us. That is an erroneous concept. Again I reiterate that the entire universe wasn't for us exclusively but rather its primary intended design is for God's pleasure. John 14 tells us that He is preparing a place for us because He wants us with Him. This proves that He loves us beyond compare but we mustn't become brattish about it. It's not all about us. In fact, it really is ALL about Him. His love and grace extended to us is an act of kindness. He wants us to join Him in what He does. When we do, we will not only replace the missing angels but we will be the glorious victors of Heaven as an expression of God's extreme superiority over the foolish trifling's of Satan. This battle is far more intense than we can see. There is no doubt that high powered warfare is taking place in the unseen realm of the supernatural. Here's how we activate His battle plans.

- By virtue of God's rightful position, we know that He made the rules of engagement in this clash of powers. All sides must play by them. The Bible clearly covers all these rules. The advantage is ours since as born again believers, we now have the power of the Holy Spirit and His physical presence living within our spirit beings.

- Some of these rules include, born again humans would take part in the warfare process through prayer, fasting, self-denial and worship to God no matter what the circumstances. Underestimating the power of prayer is like doubting the firepower of an F-16 fighter jet. God often activates a host of angels when we pray, e.g., Acts 12-5-17. Peter went to jail and as a result the church prayed all night. Only then was the angel activated. It would seem that some of these angels are obligated to wait until we pray. This could easily be part of the prescribed *terms of war*. This doesn't make us the boss of the war but it does give us permission to engage it on God's side with God's authority. He *IS* the Boss! However, we **must** engage! It is intriguing that God would allow us such a vital role in the process.

- Satan hates it when we pray. He works diligently around the clock to keep us from the act of prayer. He preoccupies us with his tricks and distractions. He feeds us a continual diet of unbelief from a world bent on nullifying the reality of God's existence.

- Fasting enables us to break through the barriers of the flesh and activate our spiritual side by way of the power of the Holy Spirit. Once we activate the power of God within us, the flesh is defeated and supernatural intervention begins.

- Christ gives us a myriad of gifts, favors and tools to accomplish our callings here on this planet. Paul instructs Timothy to "equip the saints to do ministry." Equipping them must mean that they have an assignment. With the right training, it can be extremely effective.

- The number one mistake that we make is thinking it's all about us when in fact it's all about the Father. It is very easy to get caught-up in our needs and our version of the world.

- Having a *title* is not the destination; a title should only be the result of a series of assignments done well. The assignment is *the journey* aspect of life. This morning the assignment might come in the challenge of dealing with an upset cashier but next it might be that we must face a dangerous driver on the road. How will you work that assignment? Some might think of it as a constant barrage of tests but that is **not** a correct perspective. Our experiences in life are simply a series of assignments to establish the Kingdom of God on this planet. We should consider it to be a privilege to be soldiers of the Cross. You see if we believe everything is a test that merely proves we believe it is all about us but if we believe *life* is an assignment that means that we believe it is all about the Kingdom of God. Which do you believe is true? He isn't testing us; He believes in us and has sent us to do His work. This ongoing idea that God constantly wonders about our commitment is humanistic and pitiful. He already knows us. He doesn't have to test us to find out things about us. We are soldiers on assignment and He sends us to conquer the territory for His Kingdom. What would happen if we suddenly realized that life is not about testing us but rather it is about sending us? What if we find it is His intention to send light into the midst of darkness? Consider the possibilities of being a part of the plan to bring His truth to a broken world. What if that was His plan all along? You see, it really isn't about us after all. It is about us being on assignment to establish His ways, His thoughts and His

The Plan

1   leadership in a lost and dying world. This concept is
2   a real game changer!

Chapter 3
The Plan

Key Word Studies in Context

<u>Imps</u> – (Pg. 25, #18), a young, inferior demon, a little, malignant spirit, a puny demon, a contemptible evil worker.

<u>Hypothesis</u> – (Pg. 25, #20), an educated guess based on available fact, not necessarily conclusive but probable.

<u>Evidentiary</u> - (Pg. 25, #20), as based on evidence, proof of fact.

<u>Precept</u> – (Pg. 25, #21) an established doctrine and sound biblical overview of truth.

<u>Protagonistic</u> – (Pg. 25, #27), an attitude or action of one who is a supporter, admirer, booster or friend, an advocate or champion of a cause or course of action.

<u>Auspices</u> – (Pg. 27, #26), having protection, guidance by way of authority over something.

<u>Nephilim</u> – (Pg. 27, #36), Believed to be an antediluvian (before the flood) hybrid race with the blending of humans and fallen angels. Also, some scholars think that these are the "Giants" to which Joshua and Caleb referred when they spied out the land. Goliath and his brothers believed to be a part of this hybrid race. Many believe that eliminating or impeding their influence and apparent proliferation (increase in numbers) is the primary reason for the world-wide flood.

<u>Plausible</u> – (Pg. 28, #5), reasonable or believable.

<u>Empirical</u> – (Pg. 28, #6), derived from or guided by experience or experiment.

<u>Propagate</u> – (Pg. 30, #31), to grow, extend or increase.

Workbook Activities

1. The most overlooked fact that helps to establish the foundation to an understanding about this is that the war between God and Satan is still raging. Explain this in detail. (Pg. 25, #4-14)

2. What was Lucifer's role in Heaven? (Pg. 25, #16-34; Pg. 26, #1-18)

3. What was the reason for Lucifer's fall? (Pg. 26, #19-35)

4. Discuss what we know of Satan's fall from Heaven. (Pg. 27, #1-8)

5. When Satan was cast out of Heaven, where did he go? (Pg. 27, #9-12)

6. In theory, what are the respective roles of the primary angels? (Pg. 27, #13-30)

7. What is the basic *theory* behind the land of Nod and the Nephilim? (Pg. 27, #31-36; Pg. 28, #1-8)

8. Jesus taught us that our lives should consist of worship of the father both by instruction and example. Why would we come to this conclusion? (Pg. 28, #9-16)

9. What did Jesus do about Satan's plan to corrupt God's destiny for mankind? (Pg. 28, #17-26)

10. Why does Satan hate humans so much? (Pg. 28, #27-36; Pg. 29, #1-36; Pg. 30, #1-4)

11. Compare the temptations of Adam with the temptations of Christ. (Pg. 30, #5-13)

12. Why did Jesus come to earth? (Pg. 30, #14-18)

13. What was Jesus' gift to us that guarantees our success? (Pg. 30, #19-21)

14. If God is so great then why are we still dealing with war, hunger and earthly struggles? (Pg. 30, #22-29)

15. Why were we born? (Pg. 30, #30-34)

16. How does it change our view of life if we see ourselves as soldiers sent into a war zone with an end goal in mind? (Pg. 31, #1-3)

17. Not only are we the redeemed, but we are a part of the redemptive mechanism for the fallen souls of people and to establish the Kingdom of God on planet earth. Discuss how this changes our reason to be here and why the lost need us to do our assignments. How is our obedience a spiritual act of piercing the darkness? (Pg. 31, #4-10)

18. Are we the only reason Jesus came to earth? Explain your answer. (Pg. 31, #12-32)

19. Who wrote the rules of engagement and who must follow them? (Pg. 31, #34-36; Pg. 32, #1-4)

20. What are some of the ways that we are to engage in war? Can you think of others? (Pg. 32, #5-20)

21. How does Satan gain an advantage by preoccupying or entangling us in life's issues? (Pg. 32, #21-25)

22. How does getting the flesh under control make us available to the Holy Spirit? Name some examples. (Pg. 32, #26-30)

23. One of the primary duties of a pastor and church is to "equip the saints to do ministry." What does this mean and have we operated that way in the past? (Pg. 32, #31-36)

24. It is critical to discover that we are not here for us but rather we are here to serve the Lord and worship the Father. Discuss what it means to have the *right motive* at the very core of who we are and why we should. (Pg. 33, #1-4)

25. People who seek for titles miss the main thing. They see it as a destination but in truth, it's all about the journey. That's the good stuff! Explain why that is. (Pg. 33, #5-35; Pg. 34, #1-2)

Chapter 4
Vulnerability

It is difficult to know why we are here if we search for that answer in jobs, relationships and ownership of things. We can't find the answer there. By its very nature, this urgent search for significance drives us to self-protect. That complicates the issue all the more. It closes us off to the very thing we need. It stops us from being open and vulnerable to those who could do us the most good and more importantly, it stops us from being open to God. We are somehow afraid to let go and give Him the reigns for fear that we might not like His version of life for us. Let's face it; we're living in a world where being vulnerable is perceived as a weakness. After all that does mean that someone may have an advantage over us in some way. However I contend that in a marriage relationship, one cannot be truly in love without being vulnerable. Oh, we may love someone without it but the distinction here is being "in-love." Fully surrendering to your spouse means that you must trust that they will not harm you when you are most vulnerable. You give them your total heart happily because you fully believe that they will guard it with complete care and respect. It is impossible to be *fully* "in-love" unless one can experience this depth of trust. I suppose that one could argue that there may be varying degrees of love or measure incremental levels of trust but I believe before one can truly experience the fullest expression of marriage, vulnerability must be there in full force. Vulnerability simply means trust. No one can know what it is to be "in-love" without complete trust.

At this point you may be wondering why being vulnerable has anything to do with our divine assignments. We must completely learn to trust His judgement for

1   direction in our lives before we can serve the Lord with
2   unwavering faithfulness. Let's consider what it means to
3   *refuse* to be vulnerable with the Lord. It means that we are
4   in the self-protect mode. This also indicates that we have
5   disabled our trust factor. While there may be varying degrees
6   of trust, we know that God requires ***all*** of our being to use us
7   fully in His service. This may be the most ***authentic*** truth yet
8   concerning our allegiance to Him. Have you ever heard the
9   saying, "If He's not Lord of all, He's not Lord at all?" God
10   will not accept any other Gods before Him *or* alongside of
11   Him. We must take the plunge and dive in head first. This is
12   evidence of a love relationship that is healthy. If we are not
13   healthy, then we should address that so that the Lord can do
14   the emotional surgery necessary to get us on the right track.
15   Unfortunately, people often don't go there and assume their
16   limited trust is acceptable but it is not. It can be a starting
17   place but it cannot be where we set up housekeeping. The
18   more vulnerable we are with Him, the more usable we
19   become. It really is that simple.
20
21   Self-protection by its very nature limits access from
22   the outside. A marriage won't survive it if it remains static
23   and refuses to change. This holds true with a static
24   relationship with God. The entire premise of a relationship
25   is about change. A "static" relationship means it remains
26   unchanged and isn't evolving. Every relationship needs to
27   flourish by growing and developing into something more
28   than it was yesterday. This requires mutual effort by both
29   parties. God's nature is to operate this way. He sends His
30   sweet Spirit to woo us and draw us near Him. *We* have to
31   make a deliberate effort to reciprocate and pursue Him
32   otherwise we remain self-contained, ***devoid*** of the exciting
33   hope of a brighter tomorrow.
34
35   I have a powerful saying – "love deliberately." That
36   simply suggests that we must intentionally invest in others.

1   This kind of pro-active perspective is what changes lives,
2   both ours and those with whom we invest our love. While it
3   is true, loving others means we become vulnerable to them,
4   I want to quote a famous poet here for you. Alfred Lord
5   Tennyson wrote, "'Tis better to have loved and lost than
6   never to have loved at all." To understand this fully, it is
7   beneficial to weigh out the cost of loneliness compared to a
8   heart that has loved and lost. Both are fundamentally the
9   same, only the one with the broken heart has at least
10 experienced knowing love. Therefore based upon that logic,
11 the worst tragedy of all would be to have never known love
12 at all. What we all gain from the "love" experience alone is
13 worth whatever pain that might come along with the
14 relationship. The concept just accentuates the positive and
15 places the value there. I agree with Tennyson's assessment
16 with one minor caveat. When we risk all with God, we
17 ALWAYS win and we receive a love that never disappoints.
18 It is fulfilling and satisfying. It never cheats, lies, hurts or
19 damages our hearts. It is edifying, strengthening and
20 encouraging. So where is the risk in falling in love with
21 Jesus? We can trust Him. He always works things for our
22 good, according to His purposes (Romans 8:28). He has our
23 backs. He loves us and longs to develop a strong relationship
24 that is ever growing. His grace and mercy is what allows this
25 all to be possible.
26
27   Without this love relationship, how can we ever
28 know what His plan for our lives might be? How can we
29 walk in an assignment if it is intended for only those that are
30 *crazy* in love? Without this depth of love and dedication, we
31 only feel distant, alone and disconnected. We feel that
32 "Christianity" doesn't work. The aloof and distant kind of
33 Christianity commonly espoused by the world is little more
34 than emotional huff and puff and lots of fluff. The problem
35 may be that we either don't realize that the Christ experience
36 is supposed to be ***exponentially*** more or we may need to look

1 at the possibility that we have never truly met Him. Was your
2 conversion experience a radical turn from old thinking? Was
3 it dramatic enough to steal your heart? Can you go through
4 the entire day without it crossing your mind? Are you hungry
5 to know Him better? The answer to these and other similar
6 questions might well reveal your true status with the Lord.
7 The intention of this commentary is not to condemn or
8 negatively criticize anyone. Rather, the intention is to
9 present a clear picture of the radical effects of *actually*
10 *knowing Jesus.* A relationship with Him is addicting,
11 compelling and satisfying. Salvation doesn't come to us
12 simply because we think it is a good idea. The revelation of
13 Jesus comes to us by way of the Holy Spirit. It is a
14 supernatural occurrence. We don't repent simply because we
15 have been bad. We repent because the Holy Spirit has
16 revealed to us that we are sinners. Further, He reveals sin to
17 us in the way that He sees it; not based on our current moral
18 perceptions. To some, sin might be something as simple as
19 walking into a bar. To others, sin might be telling a lie. We
20 all have our ideas of what is right or wrong. The beauty of
21 being the recipient of the conviction of the Holy Spirit as He
22 unveils truth in the written Word is that God reveals sin to us
23 **from His point of view.** Generally, this revelation has more
24 to do with the attitude of the heart than it does with the
25 practical actions of sin. Once the attitude of the heart is pure,
26 identifying sin from God's perspective becomes very clear
27 and our actions naturally radically change. As we learn how
28 to perceive His voice, we change even more. There are some
29 basic rules of the game, including the biblical reference to
30 "refrain from the very appearance of evil." Clearly this
31 doesn't allow us cart-blanch permission to do whatever our
32 flesh desires. That would be entirely backward. We are to
33 seek the leadership of the Holy Spirit and the written Word
34 to guide us into right decisions. **Only God truly knows that**
35 **which offends His Holiness.** We should diligently inquire
36 about that before we act. That's what we should think of

1 before we make decisions on our own. Sin always begins
2 with an attitude. An attitude begins with a decision. If we
3 keep our attitudes in check and compare them to the wishes
4 of the Holy Spirit and His Word, we will much more easily
5 follow the leading of the Lord. In so doing we will always
6 be fulfilled and greatly favored in spiritual matters. The flesh
7 will forcefully battle for rulership but it has no right to win.
8 God's purposes are always greater.
9
10   It is hard to imagine that we could know our place in
11 this world without first knowing Jesus very well. After all
12 He made everything including us. He knows exactly what
13 we need. In fact He is already in the future so it would be
14 foolish to presume that He is ever surprised about anything.
15 He knows what we need for tomorrow so He prepares us for
16 it today. I'm glad He is the one who knows what's in my
17 future. I don't think I really want to know. It would be a
18 hopeless feeling if I thought that I had no involvement at all
19 in my future. The truth is from God's point of view, it's
20 already a done deal. Everything that will be already is from
21 where He sits. However from our point of view being
22 naturally bound by time, we have the luxury of feeling that
23 we are *intrinsically* involved in that which happens in our
24 lives. Both views are correct. It really is the age-old
25 argument of whether predestination is a correct perspective.
26 Free will is simply man's view which is a finite view.
27 Predestination is God's view which is infinite. Both views
28 are biblically correct. We can't shock God or surprise Him
29 in any way and yet He made it possible for us to engage life
30 with decisions and hope for a change. In the dimension of
31 time, this holds true and is solid at its premise but in God's
32 view, it's all a done deal. By God's Grace, as evangelicals
33 we get to make choices but let us never forget that they are
34 never a surprise to God. He already knows. Predestination
35 does not negate the need for us to evangelize the world since
36 that is indeed the plan of God so that the world can hear His

1 message. Therefore we are engaged in the sovereign will of
2 God when we share the Gospel, just as He expected.
3 However to us it just feels like we get to choose. We do
4 whatever we do and still God knows it all before we do it.
5 It's really not all that complicated after all, is it? If someone
6 asks me if I believe in *predestination*, my answer is always
7 yes, but not without the doctrine of *free will*. If someone asks
8 me if I believe in the doctrine of *free will*, my answer is
9 always yes but not without *predestination*. Again, both are
10 correct at the same time. If we cannot trust God and be
11 vulnerable with Him, how can we know Him? He holds the
12 future. He has a plan. Our job is to walk in it and live life
13 abundantly. If we cannot believe that He made it possible for
14 us to engage Him with our will, why try? We can live a life
15 of expectation and hope AND fulfill the sovereign
16 predestined will of God at the same time. Both are necessary
17 for us at some level to experience His nature. He has made
18 this available to us as an act of grace. If our assignments were
19 determined before we were born as proponents of
20 predestination believe, then we must trust in the fact that he
21 has a clear path for us to accomplish. My goal is to obey His
22 perfect will and watch Him work His Kingdom business. I
23 heard someone argue that predestination was a false doctrine
24 because he said that he could go jump in front of a car at any
25 time. I laughingly said, "Yes but God knew you were going
26 to be stupid before you were born!" You just can't out think
27 God. He is already there. Jesus said in John 8:47-59, "Before
28 Abraham was I am." He was already in the future and still is
29 today. Trust Him. He knows what He is doing. Be diligent
30 about your spiritual duties and fulfill the assignment that
31 God has for you. Remember that from our earthly view, we
32 can work hard for Jesus or we can spend a lifetime trying to
33 live out a permanent vacation. Either way, God already
34 knows the decisions we will make concerning our lives. We
35 might as well make a decision to be all that we can be for
36 Him. That is what boosts the Kingdom. If we are slothful and

1 lazy, God already knows that too. Why not choose life and
2 let THAT be your destiny. Does this make sense to you? If I
3 get to choose in large part how I live my life then let me
4 choose to serve God faithfully with heart-felt dedication.
5 Simply because God already knows our decisions before we
6 make them doesn't stop us from making them. He knew we
7 would so He's expecting it. Keep in mind that we live in a
8 time ***continuum***. God lives where there is no such thing as
9 time. It can be challenging wrapping our heads around this
10 but once we do, it is freeing to know that we are safe with
11 Him.

Chapter 4
Vulnerability

Key Word Studies in Context

<u>Vulnerability</u> – (Pg. 42, #2), capable of being hurt: willing to be open without fear of reprisal.

<u>Authentic</u> – (Pg. 43, #7), not false or copied, true: genuine or accurate.

<u>Devoid</u> – (Pg. 43, #32), not having: being empty or without.

<u>Exponentially</u> – (Pg. 44, #36), to produce rapidly or in large quantities.

<u>Intrinsically</u> – (Pg. 46, #23), belonging to a thing by its very nature, built in value or purpose.

<u>Continuum</u> – (Pg. 48, #8), anything that gradually goes from one state to another: without discontinuing or having abrupt changes.

Workbook Activities

1. What hinders us most from being vulnerable?
   (Pg. 42, #4-31)

Vulnerability

2. Why is being vulnerable necessary to fulfill our assignments? (Pg. 42, #33-35; 43, #1-19)

3. Why is it necessary for relationships to evolve? (Pg. 43, #21-33)

4. Risking all that we have is always safe with God. Discuss the reasons why this is true. (Pg. 43, #35-36; Pg. 44, #1-25)

5. If our flesh has its way, it will defeat our assignments. Discuss how this happens and what we can do about it. (Pg. 44, #27-36; Pg. 45, #1-36; Pg. 46, #1-8)

6. God is in the past, present and the future. Discuss what that means to each of us. (Pg. 46, #10-36; Pg. 47, #1-36; Pg. 48, #1-11)

Chapter 5
Learning the Art of Enduring Well

It seems unlikely that anyone would be willing to suffer without a known purpose. In fact everything in us seeks to avoid suffering in every way. Most people spend an entire lifetime working feverishly to avoid any and all discomfort. This quest is often the ongoing **mantra** of our western society. If we were to sit back and watch this common behavior as the proverbial *fly on the wall*, we would be thoroughly entertained. The extreme if not comical efforts that some people go through are amusing to say the least. These days when someone does not get his or her way, they often perceive it as suffering. At first glance it is laughable but the truth is we have become weak and silly in our perspective of life's common woes.

Most people that go through difficulty find that they are not very well equipped for it. Their mental status is ill-prepared and they really don't comprehend the full scope of hardship. Americans in particular have a high level of difficulty with negotiating disappointment. While it is true that most of us have gone through our fair share of it, we often do so kicking and screaming the entire time. That behavior subverts the actual value of the experience. Some of us respond by getting angry with God and turning our backs on Him completely. This is a painful and destructive behavior. It is also indicative of spiritual immaturity. There is no question that we all need to grow in a lot of areas but we should never allow or tolerate our own rebellion. You can see the selfishness on the highway in the way that people drive their cars. They are often ego-centric and instantly angered when things don't go their way. We have created an entire generation of whinny-babies. We live in a time where we don't want to offend anybody so everybody gets a trophy

1   in a softball game. We believe that suffering at the smallest
2   level is a cruel and abusive experience. It's all rather silly.
3   It's okay to suffer and our children need to know how to do
4   that too. Without it, they are devoid of experience and
5   knowledge. Pain gives us a certain appreciation for relief.
6
7   Conversely, suffering well is not the total answer to
8   life's dilemmas. When we suffer (we all do), we must
9   comprehend its intrinsic value. It teaches us to be tough and
10   to make conscious efforts to endure well. The one very
11   obvious thing about our modern society is that our response
12   is to complain because we're not the boss of life. This is not
13   at all wholesome or healthy for us as a society or as a
14   Christian people. The very foundation of our faith is born
15   from suffering. All of the disciples died cruel and painful
16   deaths except for John the brother of James. However his
17   enemies did try to boil him in oil. The Lord did not hesitate
18   to remind us that He suffered and so shall we (John 16:33).
19
20   Disappointment can be a good medicine in the right
21   doses. Too much can cause damage but when given in the
22   right amount, it can keep us grounded. It should remind us
23   to never forget the mercy that was extended to us.
24   Disappointment and **hardship** is the mirror that we face
25   every day. When our neighbor buys a new car and we can't
26   afford the light bill, we get to deal with potential envy and
27   jealousy. We get to see what is inside of us and snuff it out
28   at the root. This teaches us to have patience and to bless
29   others assuming we make the right choices about our
30   feelings. It is a choice. We can choose to let envy grow or we
31   can choose to bless our neighbors and say "good for them!"
32   Disappointment can also ground us to the extent that we
33   reject being arrogant and haughty. ***However, disappointment***
34   ***alone has its limitations.*** We must not allow it to be the
35   *standard* by which we live in order to remain humble. We
36   should intentionally be humble by following the example of

1   Christ who refused to lift His own will above His Father's.
2   He came as a servant with a big-picture-focus so that the
3   world would receive the benefit of His coming. Even so
4   disappointment will come to all of us. It can be a friend or
5   an enemy. How we let it play out in our emotions will
6   determine its effects. It can beat us down to the point that we
7   have no hope OR as a result of its revelation, we can remain
8   humble, trust in the Lord and know that His plans are to bless
9   us and not to harm us (Jeremiah 29:11).

Who tells us today that we are not supposed to suffer? – Marketers! We've bought a bill of goods and along with it we have swallowed its lies, hook, line and sinker. They relentlessly remind us every day of how special we are. They tell us that we deserve the best. Our forefathers, early settlers, American Indians or for that matter, the preceding generations before us never taught us that. They all went through hardship but they stood up to it. Their personal pride and self-image found its identity based upon their ability to endure rather than from predisposed arrogance. They didn't go around whining and moaning about how life isn't *fair*. By the way, **life isn't fair**. EVERYONE will have hardships no matter your social standing or spiritual level. Life is hard. This is the result of the fall of Adam. Life is tough; expect it! The Bible is very clear about it. We are going to suffer! In fact, Jesus said to leap for joy when people speak evil of us.

We forget that enduring well as good soldiers is expected of us, "Thou therefore endure hardness, as a good soldier of Jesus Christ." (II Timothy 2:3). Also we should know that it's okay to be inconvenienced. It's okay to miss your turn in the line at Burger King because of someone's selfish attitude. It's okay to yield to someone who races to get your parking space. It's okay to prefer others above ourselves. It is part of our calling to do this. There's nothing wrong with letting someone else go first. People who struggle with this are not at peace with themselves. We should all keep in mind that we are not here for ourselves but rather for others. We are here to touch lives and to make a difference for the Kingdom of God.

The "name it and claim it" culture for some reason doesn't embrace the suffering part of Christianity. Their belief is that we are King's Kids and we have been sent here to take back the Kingdom but with one specific caveat; they believe that we can claim blessings so that we never have to struggle or endure. While I am a real proponent of the power of the believer, I do not think that we are or should be exempt from suffering. It was Jesus who said *leap for joy* when men shall revile you and speak all manner of evil against you for His sake (Matthew 5:11). There is something powerful about suffering for the cause that creates a deep abiding love for it. Getting *everything* we want just feeds our **egos** and creates a bunch of brats who are all about themselves. There is no doubt in my mind that we will do great exploits in these last days but **they will not occur without suffering**. As powerful and favored as the Apostle Paul was, he suffered greatly but kept his focus on his divine assignment nonetheless. For us to accomplish the assignment that God has given us, we must be willing to suffer and still maintain our specific purpose. Most people believe that being in God's will makes everything easy. Wow! Have they never read the Bible?

We have become soft and ego-centric. We errantly believe that the life's plan is all about us. We believe that God would never let His children go through hardship. We think, "What kind of God would do that?" Have we even *read* the Bible? We can see the beauty of our assignment once we deliberately do our assignment. The key here is for us to KNOW without a doubt that we are on an assignment. Knowing this may potentially be more powerful than doing the actual assignment. The assignment is very important to

1   say the least but there is something that deeply moves God
2   when we engage it with fervor. When we consider the
3   Apostle Paul and how he operated, one thing is clear above
4   all else; he never lost sight of his mission. They couldn't beat
5   it out of him and therefore they couldn't stop him. With
6   everything that was in him, he meant to finish his race well.
7   Here is where the grievous agony of the modern believer is
8   most notable today. We don't want to suffer for anything. We
9   think that suffering is not the will of God and so therefore
10   when we do, we believe that we are out of His will. We have
11   few things if any for which we are loyal enough to die.
12   What's worse is we have few things for which we are willing
13   to suffer *inconvenience*. Oh, I know we don't think we are
14   this way but upon closer examination, we must concede to
15   the facts. For example, most churches operate with a small
16   number of leaders. Usually the statistics fall between 5% and
17   20% of a given church congregation. It is no surprise that
18   Christianity is unapologetically under attack on a daily basis
19   as though a steam roller ran it over. People that stand
20   peacefully at abortion clinics, do jail ministries or witness to
21   folks on the street are sadly **castigated** as eccentrics or
22   radicals. If a believer goes to jail for his faith which happens
23   more than we think, we treat them as weird, unwise or as
24   some kind of religious fanatic. Just think of it this way. If we
25   were to interview the Apostle Paul for a lead pastor role or
26   for that matter any of the disciples, we wouldn't hire any of
27   them. After all, these are *jail-bird fanatics* that stir up trouble
28   all the time. With the exception of Paul, none of them had
29   seminary degrees including Jesus. They were mostly ruffians
30   and didn't hold a particularly high standing in the
31   community. Nowadays pastors have to be perfect with a
32   "can't we all just get along" attitude. God forbid that a pastor
33   would preach with the fire of John the Baptist and have the
34   unabashed boldness of Peter! Oh, that we would have bold
35   believers who would stir up the world and force them to
36   awaken from their comatose state to see the beauty of that

1 which Jesus brings! The consuming fire of God found in
2 Hebrews 12:29 refers to a fire that creates a purging and a
3 cleansing process of fire. It literally turns everything in its
4 path into itself; fire! This must happen to us all!
5
6   In a football game, the opposing team's primary goal
7 is to make the other team forget how much they want to win.
8 They will pound away making them believe that winning is
9 not possible. Young players may not overtly realize that this
10 is their primary goal but that is exactly what coaches want to
11 accomplish in the minds of each of his players. They must
12 weaken the opposing team's resolve to win. If you don't
13 really want to win strongly enough, you will give up
14 relatively easily. Once the clock starts, the real game of
15 intimidation begins, often unseen by the crowd.
16 Conversations are going on at the line. Growling and eye
17 contact ensues. Then the snap takes place and they clash with
18 great force! With strength and intimidation, each team seeks
19 to score. Power, skill and smart plays are all meaningful tools
20 in the game of football. In fact they are all necessary.
21 However, none of these compare to the *will* to win. If you
22 somehow alter the opposition's will to win, they become
23 vulnerable and as a result, beaten. If they have all the skills
24 needed but they *don't believe* they can win, do you think they
25 will? Their opposing team would have to be terrible not to
26 beat them in such a case. In the end, after normal game
27 preparation, winning boils down to how they believe. If we
28 can't see ourselves winning, then it is highly unlikely that
29 we will. If we do not have a desire to win no matter what,
30 then we won't. It stands to reason why Satan works on the
31 human mind so much, accusing, intimidating and
32 demoralizing us all seemingly at will. His goal is to
33 convince us to throw in the towel; don't!
34
35   The Old Testament teaches us to "meditate" upon
36 God's Word and His ways but most of us do not really know

1 what that means. According to Strong's Concordance, the
2 word "meditate" means to *imagine*. So if I think of what His
3 Word says and I imagine it coming to be, then I have truly
4 come into agreement with it. As a result, I become part of the
5 solution rather than the opposition. The Bible further teaches
6 us to adjust our brains to God's thinking all the time, e.g.,
7 "think on these things…" (Philippians 4:8). This is not New
8 Age thinking. This is how God taught us to think. "As a man
9 thinks in his heart, so is he… (Proverbs 23:7)" I have never
10 done home construction where I didn't first see the finished
11 product in my mind. In fact, you can't even draw it out on
12 paper without first imagining it. In order to accomplish our
13 assignments, we must first believe that we are on an
14 assignment. Then we must prepare as God provides training
15 (as needed). Then we must see ourselves as able to do that
16 which God is asking us to do. After all, He hasn't sent us to
17 do His work alone. He provides us with none other than the
18 amazing and extremely powerful Holy Spirit. He will
19 perform His wonders as needed. We simply become His
20 connection to the natural via our bodies, moving, talking,
21 singing, laughing, witnessing or whatever it is that He has
22 sent us to do. Satan knows this and attacks us at that point.
23 He throws up all our negative history and failures and tells
24 us we are worthless. His appeal is to our flesh. When he does
25 that, we tend to agree with his assessment and therefore we
26 do nothing. We must believe that we can do what God
27 designed us to do. We are equipped by way of the power of
28 the Holy Spirit. Most often, we simply lack the will. The
29 belief that we can succeed is not there. We've been robbed!
30 We have no will to stand up and fight for the right cause that
31 will stand throughout eternity. We've been had!
32
33 We've been undermined, outwitted and intimidated.
34 That alone should give us cause to be angry as hornets! God
35 sent us here to do a specific job. What is stopping us? More
36 importantly, what in particular is stopping you? Are we

1 fearful of pain, inconvenience and obligation? That sounds
2 more like an intimidated male that is fearful of commitment
3 in a relationship. Are we worried that we won't be able to
4 pursue our life of fun anymore? Is it possible that we have
5 given up our ability to endure and be strong in exchange for
6 convenience and fun? Are we that easy? Are we so gullible
7 that we have forfeited things that are eternal for things that
8 are fleeting and temporary? Yes we are. Conversely, having
9 "fun" is not the enemy here. God gave us pleasure to
10 experience joy and to appreciate the value of living.
11 However, pleasure should never get in the way of our eternal
12 destiny and purpose of being. Here is a list of things that will
13 help us to keep our focus on our true purpose.
14
15 • Toughen up and stop whining about every
16   inconvenience that comes along.
17 • Be willing to endure wrongs by others and let it go.
18 • Hold to the idea that you are here for a purpose. That
19   purpose is more about a lot of small assignments
20   instead of one big assignment as many think. Believe
21   that you must live out your assignment and NEVER
22   let it go.
23 • Get your head straight on the subject of winning. We
24   were born to win but the enemy has learned how to
25   get us off track. Wise up and become pro-active,
26   recognizing his pernicious activities.
27 • Stop loving the world more than you love God.
28   Satan's plan is a vortex that sucks you up and then
29   drops you into its compelling free fall, up then down,
30   over and over. At that point you think that escaping
31   such a vicious cycle is not an option because you
32   believe that this is normal. What a lie!
33 • Know that God did not send you here alone. He
34   provides all the equipment but you must walk in faith
35   (divine persuasion). Just do it! Satan knows how to
36   stop us from accessing that power. This nullifies the

call of God and puts it so far on the back burner that it is never a threat to his evil plans.

- Be tenacious like a Pit Bull dog. Get a bite and don't let go! Believe that your purpose is vital to the Kingdom. Get some **backbone**.
- Endure well.
- Know that your strength alone is incapable of battle. We must KNOW the Lord and learn of His ways. Study His Word, fast often to keep the flesh under control and pray constantly. He will use you and your faith will grow. Believe it!
- Know that God's plans are HUGE! We can be a part of it as this is the most exciting time to live in the history of the world!

Understanding the power of your assignment is indeed a game changer! No one can persevere through difficulty without having a powerful reason to do so. **Enduring well is a matter of believing more in the cause than being concerned about the pain.** This leads us to a dilemma. Most people only know Christ as an acquaintance. They know Him by name, recognize Him when they see Him but they've never been out to eat with Him and they haven't invited Him to come over. They don't recognize the kinship with him and consequently have not become vulnerable with Him. Just as they treat a plumber or an electrician, they only call him when they need him. They think He's a nice guy and does good work but He always wants money. This really is how some people see Jesus. They drop Him like a hot potato the minute He is no longer convenient or on the hotlist of things to do. They only go to church when nothing else is going on, e.g., vacation, day at the lake, going out of town, nephew's birthday party and so on. No wonder suffering for Christ is to them a silly concept. They think that people who do are fanatics and maybe even weirdos. If our *Christian* world is mostly made of this kind of individual, who then will complete the assignment of establishing the Kingdom of God on this planet? If Jesus is a mere social convenience and a conscience buffer, why suffer when a glass of wine will do just as well? That's the way some people think. That is a powerful question nonetheless. I just want to say, *we need some* **backbone**! There's nothing more disgusting than a person who is like water which by nature always flows to the lowest point! The fact is that I wouldn't be willing to suffer or die for just a good idea but I would die for my wife and children. I would die for my parents although they have already gone ahead of me. To make it all more personal, let me say it from my own perspective. If there was no kinship with Jesus, He wouldn't be on my list of people to die for either. Because there is a true kinship, His cause IS my cause. His will is my directive. His Kingdom is my assignment. I owe Him everything! This does not automatically make us weird or freaks because we want to do good in the world. It does mean that we recognize that there are purposes bigger than our soccer games and concert goings. If we do these things, let us never ignore the assignments intertwined in them. This means that for us to know His full purpose in life we must look outside our own little world's and see that the Kingdom of God is HUGE. His plans trump our own. He joyfully lets us live our lives but He never stops the assignments simply because we are not in the church building at the moment. The good thing is that our assignments are for the good of all. When we pursue His plans, He provides hope for the broken, food for the hungry and an eventual destination to be with Him forever. Again, I reiterate that family, fun and pleasure is not a negative subject, neither should it be thought of as wrong. However in this life, we can get our priorities confused with the current happenings and miss out on the big picture. We should love our families and minister to them as well. The point is life can't be just about things as millions of modern families think today. God's picture must guide us.

1   The beauty is that there are indeed people who do get
2 it and they have established a true relationship with the real
3 Jesus of the Bible rather than some sicky-sweet media
4 version. The true Jesus of the Bible has more than enough
5 compassion to go around but while He first came as our
6 Savior, He will return as the Judge. The Scriptures are clear
7 about that. People then can say, "You're not supposed to
8 judge all they want" but the fact remains; He is coming back
9 for that very reason. What will they say then, "Oops?"

Chapter 5
Learning the Art of Enduring Well

Key Study Words in Context

<u>Mantra</u> – (Pg. 51, #8), a word or repeated over and over, that which represents your song or word.

<u>Hardship</u> – (Pg. 52, #24), tough times, difficulty, things that greatly challenge us.

<u>Fair</u> – (Pg. 53, #21), equal, equitable, balanced, having equal treatment.

<u>Ego</u> – (Pg. 54, #17), the central thought process of self.

<u>Castigated</u> – (Pg. 55, #21), to criticize, punish or rebuke severely.

<u>Backbone</u> – (Pg. 60, #6), strength, fortitude, willingness to endure, a refusal to surrender.

Workbook Activities

1. How does being at peace with one's self make life sweeter? (Pg. 51, #4-16)

2. Selfishness is the enemy to the believer. Discuss the reasons why this is. (Pg. 51, #18-35; Pg. 52, #1-5)

3. What did Jesus say about His followers suffering? (Pg. 52, #7-18)

4. Discuss the ways in which disappointment can be both a friend and an enemy. (Pg. 52, #20-36; Pg. 53, #1-9)

5. Life is not fair. Discuss why this is and determine why it doesn't matter. (Pg. 53, #11-26)

6. Discuss the benefits that can come from being inconvenienced. (Pg. 53, #28-36; Pg. 54, #1-4)

7. Does the Bible teach us that we are exempt from suffering? Please explain you answer. (Pg. 54, #6-26)

8. Why do we need the fire of God today?
   (Pg. 54, #28-36; Pg. 55, #1-36; Pg. 56, #1-4)

9. Why is having a will to win important to a believer?
   (Pg. 56, #6-33)

10. Discuss the biblical way to imagine the Word and its benefits. (Pg. 56. #35-36; Pg. 57, #1-31)

11. Think about ways that might improve your view of life and further your assignment. Explain your discoveries.
    (Pg. 57, #33-36; Pg. 58, #1-36; Pg. 59, #1-36;
    Pg. 60, #1-36)

12. What is Jesus' role when He returns to the earth and how will that affect us? (Pg. 61, #1-9)

Chapter 6
The Inability to *Cope*

The inability or unwillingness to cope has become epidemic among our people today. This directly affects their ability to endure. The world has learned to use outside mechanisms to help them to get through things. Drinking, drugs, sex or other emotional *pseudo*-supports serve as tools for getting by. This means that many if not most have rejected the normal methods of coping such as dealing with issues head-on and making proactive decisions about life. After all, they think why deal with issues when alcohol makes you feel so good and temporarily pushes off the effects of life? Their idea is to never deal with an issue so it seems that it is nonexistent. It is a foolish concept but is nonetheless very popular. It's the proverbial ostrich burying its head in the sand. Sheep do something similar. When they are under attack, they put their heads together in a big circle. It would seem that they do not wish to face their *predator*. This behavior does not change the inevitable outcome. One or more of them will be lunch for the wild beast who gleefully selects his prey without the first hint of resistance.

I once watched a very interesting video where a lioness was about to attack and eat a water buffalo. She had a clear advantage as she pounced on the seemingly defenseless animal. The water buffalo was about to go down when one of the nearby bulls began to angrily charge the lioness. Suddenly there were other water buffalos joining in support of their weakened family member. They collectively charged the lioness. She knew she couldn't take on all of them so she loosened her vicious bite and fended for her own life. Finally, she ran away. They had won because they stood together. That would certainly give us all a feeling of comfort if we would defend one another in the same way. If we all

1 did this for one another perhaps some of us would be less
2 inclined to use artificial means to get through life.
3
4   Drugs and obsessive behavior can be a challenge for
5 many people. The erroneous belief that vices can somehow
6 make life better is a pie-in-sky kind of thinking. It simply is
7 not true. Some people deliberately stay drunk because they
8 cannot cope with life. They believe that being drunk gets
9 them through it and therefore they become not only
10 physically addicted, they become emotionally addicted as
11 well. It's all a lie. It only *seems* to help but the reality is that
12 the problems are still there after they sober-up. In their
13 minds, that's all the more reason to remain drunk. When they
14 do this, they miss out on life and what's more, they miss out
15 on their true reason to be. Their assignment goes unattended
16 and before they know it, life goes by unnoticed and then it's
17 all over.
18
19   There is something tragically lost by deferring to
20 other methods of coping rather than standing up to the
21 challenges in life. The one that lives this way misses out on
22 experiencing personal victory or what it is like to persevere
23 to the point of true success. We have reared a generation to
24 believe that *suffering* is the enemy so they pursue comfort as
25 though that is their purpose in life. If that philosophy is
26 strong enough, this kind of thinker believes that they have
27 no value without pleasure. They have learned to measure the
28 value of life based on how good they have it. If that doesn't
29 meet their expectations, they feel less valuable and therefore
30 insignificant. Anything that comes along that opposes or
31 challenges their hope for success makes them feel as though
32 they are cursed. As a result, they believe their life can never
33 be what they want it to be so it leaves them feeling broken
34 and empty. How can they cope with it if they have
35 abandoned the emotional skills that God put in them?
36 Perhaps they have no experience using them and as such

these supernatural skills seem to be nonexistent. Either way, the end result is the same. This holds true for the believer as well. We may have gifts but if they remain in the box under the tree, they do us no good. In this case, they turn to other things because they are seekers of pleasure. Rather than standing flat footed and saying enough is enough and refusing to allow vices to rule, substitutions are easy to get so convenience wins out.

Many of these opt for a no faith kind of lifestyle. After all, who needs faith when you can simply pop a top and the pain doesn't exist for a while? If that's not enough, *they just do more* until they don't have to cope at any level. Their lifestyle then turns to an addiction driven craving to find the next fix rather than facing and living life head-on. They literally detach themselves from life. The next thing you know, their personality is gone and all they live for is the next fix. They exist in an *extreme survival mode* because they either have no skills to cope with the challenges of life or they gave them away in exchange for an addiction. The process is tragic and the end result is antifamily and antilife. They become isolationists. Paranoia is common among these individuals. Their hopelessness, coupled with the vicious cycle of more and more chemicals prevails until the mechanism to *feel* anything is gone. All that remains is anger, impatience and an insatiable quest for more coping substitutions.

Being extremely insecure can also lead to extreme jealousy, paranoia, depression and a myriad of other emotional maladies. There are many reasons that one might turn to pornography but being emotionally insecure is most common. Watching pornography has a stimulating affect in that it can simulate the feeling of being alive even though it is not wholesome or good for anyone. It is nothing more than a fantasy that ultimately ends in utter failure and destruction.

1   It is degrading and that creates a whole new set of problems.
2   *All of the substitutions for emotions are either an attempt*
3   *to hide them or to find them.* Really think about that
4   statement. Either way, it's an out of balance emotional state
5   that leaves the individual needy. Perhaps the "hiding and the
6   finding" of emotions are more alike than we might have
7   initially thought. These are an attempt to put the emotional
8   state in a realm where we are most able to cope. What
9   happens if we don't have the skills to cope? It seems that we
10   would continue to experiment with dulling our pain by
11   pursuing emotional stimulation and excitement. Drugs and
12   alcohol are the most common substances that people use to
13   medicate themselves even though it can never truly satisfy
14   that longing inside of each of them to be significant in this
15   life. That creates a cycle of need. Even though substances do
16   not completely satisfy, they do provide a temporary reprieve.
17   That is enough for the moment for those who are used to
18   replacing coping skills with substances or things. It starts
19   with the obsession and the obsession facilitates the
20   addiction. Even people who cut themselves think that their
21   emotions are dead and cutting themselves is simply an
22   attempt to feel something, **ANYTHING**! They need to feel
23   emotional stimulation of any kind to feel alive. Experiencing
24   emotional stimulation is what makes *all of us* feel alive. It's
25   like kids who get no attention will readily accept punishment
26   in place of reward simply because it makes them feel
27   *something*. In other words, they need to feel alive and they
28   will accept it whether it is good or bad. Some kids can't get
29   attention any other way. They become addicted to getting
30   attention for doing bad things and it sets them up for a
31   lifetime of bad activity and a long string of reaping what they
32   have sown. It forms an addiction and yet they don't know
33   why they feel that way. At least for them, they feel
34   *something*. Truly, it is a sad commentary and it robs them of
35   their assignment in life. They get so preoccupied with the
36   need to *"feel"* that they spend a lifetime searching for

1 something that they will never find. The reason for this is
2 that Satan provides them with a plate full of options. All of
3 them are destructive but they do satisfy if only for the
4 moment. We have the mentality that easy is always best and
5 so we tend to live that way. If we live by this philosophy,
6 whoever offers the first enticing option can control us.
7
8   The reason why most people continue to search for
9 "feeling" is that they do not know the standard for peace and
10 therefore they cannot find **satisfaction** in that which life
11 offers them. They tend to buy the ideology that the media
12 sells them such as "You'll be happy if you buy this car or if
13 you buy this beer." If you watch these certain sports and if
14 you buy this motorcycle or boat then you will have
15 happiness. At the end of that day, all we have remaining are
16 car payments and hangovers. There must be more! How can
17 we access our assignment if we are wholly preoccupied with
18 something else? If our minds are preoccupied with self-
19 sustaining survival, how can we give ourselves to the call of
20 God? We can't. It's a pernicious trick of Satan! This is his
21 infamous sleight-of-hand routine. He preoccupies us with
22 negativities and seemingly insurmountable challenges until
23 **we become addicted to the actual preoccupation of it all**.
24 Did you catch that? He turns small issues into big ones! To
25 accomplish our assignment, we must submit ourselves to
26 God and resist the devil and if we do, the Bible declares that
27 he will flee from us (James 4:7)! "Neither give place to the
28 devil…" (Ephesians 4:27). He takes small things and makes
29 them look HUGE to us. Then we spend all of our time
30 dealing with them somewhat poorly and before we know it,
31 we have spent a lifetime caught up in the act of *coping*. How
32 clever! If we are always in the survival mode, when will we
33 do what we are here to do? When will we take on the
34 demeanor of Christ and become salt and light? If all we do
35 is spend time fretting over and examining our weaknesses
36 and flaws, when do we become soldiers?

1   Our modern culture has abandoned us. It has watched
2   us freefall into a downward spiral and then disrespectfully
3   mocks, as we lie twitching miserably on the ground. Enough
4   is enough! We must take our lives back and reject the
5   influence of a lost and immoral world. They are as lost as a
6   goose in a hurricane. Why do we care what celebrities or
7   others think? Who are they to give us their opinion about
8   what life is supposed to be? Have we lost our minds? We
9   have set up lewd *luciferians* as icons. It is painfully
10 shameful and what's more, it has left us in a tizzy of
11 pandemic proportions.
12
13   Back in the 90s I had a friend who came to me in
14 need of counseling for the addiction of pornography. He was
15 a good man but he just couldn't pull his addicted brain from
16 the scenes in his mind and from his computer. After spending
17 a considerable amount of time speaking with him about the
18 cause of such addictions, explaining the physiology of it and
19 the biblical need for being free from it, he still had
20 uncontrollable urges. He found himself compromised time
21 and time again. He finally came back to me and explained
22 his remorse for his repeated failures. I told him that I knew
23 what was wrong. He said shockingly, "What would that be?"
24 I said, "You're just not angry enough." "What do you
25 mean?" he replied. I continued, "You just haven't gotten mad
26 enough with Satan for ruling you as though you are a three
27 year old child." I further explained that no matter how
28 sophisticated counseling may be and no matter how we
29 understand the chemical responses of the brain, there's
30 ultimately one thing that frees us from our addictions and
31 that is having a hardened, stalwart attitude with a made-up
32 mind. We have to have a made up mind and have a resolve
33 that says that we are sick of it and see it for what it is: a
34 satanic ploy of distraction to keep us from our assignments!
35 God will help us with that either directly or through the help
36 of a counselor or friend. We each ought to be angry every

1   time Satan gets away with such foolishness. We must be the
2   boss of our brains and then yield them to the Holy Spirit for
3   His guidance. Who has the right to force us to do things
4   against our own wills? Paul said that we were bought with a
5   price. In other words, we don't belong to ourselves but to
6   God. We were bought and paid for. It seems foolish for Satan
7   to have control over God's property. Sometimes we have to
8   get to the point and simply say, "NO MORE!" Having
9   passion for Jesus is an exceptional tool to overcoming
10   addiction. All the counseling in the world doesn't do as much
11   good as having a godly made-up mind. Proper counseling
12   does however offer us a standard by which we can firmly
13   apply the truth of God and it can help us to make up our
14   minds to do right.

Clearly, anyone who lacks coping skills does not have a made-up mind. Their mind is already made-up *for them* via **tacit** consent by someone else. If they did, they would have a proactive plan to stand boldly against the wiles of the devil. In fact these non-coping individuals have been so cleverly undermined that largely their coping mechanisms do not exist. Oddly, they feel a sense of comfort in the addiction more than they feel the need to alleviate it. That leaves them with a life directed by whatever is most enticing at the time or by whatever soothes the broken soul *for the moment*. It is a sad state of affairs for this individual. If he finally gets to the point that he is determined to be free and will not accept no for an answer, he can do it but he should know that freedom doesn't come easily. It sometimes has to wade through the current of self-pleasure filled with exciting and pleasing **endorphin** rushes. Self-pleasure always feels good and natural but addiction pretends to be all that and much more. It is an assignment robber. It replaces freedom with feeling and momentary pleasure. The drawbacks are that it is phony, a **ruse** and a pretender. It only gives the illusion of pleasure and then only for a while. It robs the

1   individual of purpose because the addiction itself becomes
2   his or her reason to be. Then their whole world revolves
3   around that. It's nothing short of **chicanery**!
4
5   Chemicals are not the only concern here. People can
6   become addicted to their own personality traits. They can
7   become addicted to hobbies or even people for the purpose
8   of filling their brokenness inside. They can become addicted
9   to ministry as well. Sadly, it is rare that we actually identify
10 ministry addiction as an issue. It is more common than one
11 might think. There is a difference between passion and
12 addiction. These needy addicts come to believe that their
13 behavior is normal and think that's just the way life is for
14 them. Because of this, they never come to know that they
15 need to be free from such atrocities. This is a tragic way to
16 live life. The fact is most people live their lives that way.
17 That is a clever but deceptive thinking process. Unless we
18 come to the realization of its pernicious effects, we will
19 coddle it and give it permission to coexist with our spirit man
20 as though nothing is wrong. For those of us who live this
21 way, "coping" is no longer an issue due to the fact that we
22 have replaced it with our own unique personality quirks and
23 or substances that trigger pleasure. This is a clever ruse
24 indeed.

Chapter 6
The Inability to Cope

Key Word Studies in Context

1. <u>Cope</u> – (Pg. 66, #2), to effectively deal with something difficult or challenging.

2. <u>Pseudo</u> – (Pg. 66, #8), not genuine, sham, fake or pretend.

3. <u>Predator</u> – (Pg. 66, #19), something that pursues someone, an animal or a thing. Someone who intends to overcome another.

4. <u>Luciferians</u> – (Pg. 71, #9), People who follow Lucifer, evil planners, followers of satanic plans. Satan's schemers usually thought of as world dominators.

5. <u>Tacit</u> – (Pg. 72, #18), not spoken, understood or implied without being stated. Agreed to by remaining silent.

6. <u>Endorphins</u> – (Pg. 72, #31), pleasure giving hormones naturally produced by the human body. These are commonly stimulated by synthetic or artificial means as well as produced through exercise or other biological stimuli.

7. <u>Ruse</u> – (Pg. 72, #35), clever deception, a planned deception, deceitful ploy.

8. <u>Chicanery</u> – (Pg. 73, #3), deception by trickery.

Workbook Activities

1. What do many people do when they can't or won't face life? (Pg. 66, #4-22)

2. What are some of the benefits of sticking together and collectively standing against the enemy? (Pg. 66, #24-35; Pg. 67, #1-2)

3. The sad thing about turning to artificial stimulation is that people miss out on life. Explain this process and why this ends up in tragedy. (Pg. 67, #4-17)

4. What can we learn through suffering and how does that affect our assignments? (Pg. 67, #19-36; Pg. 68, #1-8)

5. When addiction takes over, the ability to be social and interactive becomes nonexistent in most cases. Why is this? What does this do to the life of the individual and to those around him? (Pg. 68, #10-27)

6. Explain what it means when we say, *"All of the substitutions for emotions are either an attempt to hide them or to find them."*
   (Pg. 68, #29-36, Pg. 69, #1-36; Pg. 70, #1-6)

7. Explain what it means to be "addicted to the actual preoccupation of it all." (Pg. 70, #8-36)

8. Explain the difference between addiction and passion. (Pg. 71, #1-36; Pg. 72, #1-14)

9. Having a made up mind can make all the difference when following Christ. Discuss what it means to have a spiritual backbone. (Pg. 72, #16-36; 73, #1-24)

Chapter 7
Superstition (More Tricks)

There are a lot of things that hinder our assignments but few have permeated the fabric of Christian thinking as much as superstition. Here's how it often goes. Many times we go through difficulties wondering what God is trying to say to us. I don't think that He tries to teach us something in every **nuance** and every **incremental** thing that happens, as some might believe. I had a friend that had a flat tire some years ago. She asked the question, "I wonder what God is trying to say in that?" I simply said, "He's trying to tell you that you need a new tire!" God is not weird or communication challenged. The success of His sovereign will is not contingent upon our ability to hear Him or to perform as some might think. He is very capable and competent when it comes to getting the job done. If God speaks to us to walk over and witness to someone standing on the corner, we tend to believe that we are their only hope. That would mean that that person's salvation is contingent upon our performance. That theological perspective is very flawed. God is not limited to the ability of man to accomplish His purposes. He knows how to get the job done with or without us. He doesn't *need* us but rather chooses to include us in what He does. He is never surprised by our actions or the lack of them, EVER! We can be so silly sometimes. Our superstitious and unbiblical concepts get in the way of God working with us more times than not. There is also ample evidence that God gives us some space to put into practice that which we have learned much the same as a good father might do with his own son. He teaches him something and then gives him room to make mistakes as he negotiates his own skills. The boy receives his father's teaching but must learn to apply it in order to have the advantage of his father's knowledge and skill.

Superstition (More Tricks)

1   There is an entire segment of the Christian culture
2 that lives in a constant superstitious state. They are so
3 desperate to *"know"* God that they see Him lurking behind
4 every rock and in every circumstance. On the one hand, God
5 instructs us to seek His face continually but on the other, He
6 teaches us to follow the Scriptures fervently in order to
7 validate that which we perceive to be His will. Validating
8 what we think He is saying is certainly a wise move. It is
9 easy to confuse the voice in our head and that which we
10 believe to be spiritual with the actual will of God. While God
11 is always present, we don't see any Scriptural evidence that
12 asserts that He cannot communicate with us in a clear and
13 present manner. There is a fundamental flaw in the idea that
14 God's first method of communication is always through
15 circumstances. If the Apostle Paul had believed that way, he
16 would have stopped what he was doing every time he faced
17 hardship which was on a daily basis. In other words,
18 superstitious believers often think that if it is God's will, it
19 will be easy. If it is not, then they believe that God will
20 communicate that by making the way hard. This is infantile
21 thinking and a ploy of Satan to dissuade us from following
22 through with our Heavenly orders. We think, "It must not be
23 God's will because nothing seems to be going our way!"
24 Welcome to real Christianity! Our service for the Lord is not
25 paved with gold. It's paved with hardship, pain and
26 suffering. Consider the martyrs of the Christian faith over
27 many centuries. Their stories are **replete** with horror and
28 agony. Why is it that our generation believes that we are
29 special and should not suffer for the cause of Christ? May I
30 venture to answer that question? It is because we are spoiled
31 and we think that we are special. We believe that the world
32 and the universe exist exclusively for us, since we are so
33 important! The fact is that we are a creation for God and His
34 pleasure. We have become spiritual brats and tend to reject
35 the idea that service to the King is supposed to be hard.
36 We've accepted an easy-peasy religion from milk-toast

1 preachers that presume comfort and convenience is the
2 standard. However, upon close inspection, it bears no
3 resemblance to the words of Jesus when He said in John
4 16:33, "In this world, you will have tribulation." Comfort is
5 found as He continues that phrase by saying, "But take
6 courage; I have overcome the world." In Him we find our
7 peace.
8
9   If we are hyper-sensitive to every incremental
10 occurrence in life believing God is saying something about
11 everything, it makes us vulnerable. Satan uses this tactic. If
12 we can't tell the difference then we're in trouble. The
13 Apostle Paul endured Satan's taunting urging him to give up
14 his God-given vision and dream. God didn't want him to quit
15 but Satan did. Satan could see that Paul had the power of
16 God upon his life and as a result, he continually buffeted
17 him. Jesus didn't take him out of it but He did take him
18 through it. If Paul had depended on circumstances to
19 determine the will of the Lord, he would have stopped dead
20 in his tracks. Who then would have written those New
21 Testament books originally penned by Paul if he had
22 determined the will of God based on what his eyes saw?
23 Astoundingly we easily operate that way. We believe if there
24 is heavy opposition then God is not in it. This begs the
25 question; where are the soldiers? Where are the warriors for
26 the faith? Are our eyes upon circumstances so much that we
27 have lost the vision for God's big picture? Peter made that
28 mistake when he walked on the water with Jesus. He got his
29 eyes on the circumstances, fear gripped him and he fell
30 helplessly into the water. Of course, Jesus stepped up and
31 saved him. What can we learn from this? Circumstances
32 always try to rise to impose themselves on our reason and
33 focus. Satan intentionally accentuates the suffering along
34 with other failures in our lives. He uses these to get our focus
35 off of the original purpose. As a result we become ego-
36 centric and forget to do God's business. Let me give you an

1 example. Writing a book seems like a fun thing to do. It is
2 exciting to see your own name on the title and be able to talk
3 about the amazing discoveries within its pages. Most people
4 are unaware of the many grueling hours of hard work it takes
5 to glean over the pages word for word and clarify every
6 thought. Then you must work endlessly to improve its
7 content knowing that even then, it may not be good enough.
8 All they see is a guy standing up in front of a crowd speaking
9 as though he's somebody but the truth is it takes a lot of hard
10 work and pain to get to that podium and that has little to do
11 with "celebrity." Bishop T. D. Jakes indicates the same thing
12 when he talks about his rise to T.V. popularity. People see the
13 glitz and glamour of being famous but they are rarely willing
14 to go through the necessary pain to have that kind of
15 platform of influence. Most people are hung up on little
16 pictures and superstition and therefore do not spiritually earn
17 the right to reach a place of high influence (Matthew 25:23).
18 God uses those who are willing to get into the trenches and
19 serve there. Our assignments should come from God and not
20 us. They certainly should not come from Satan. These people
21 who serve in high places without having a painful history
22 likely lack the skills to endure. That takes a lot of practice. It
23 takes a greater cause than our own to walk through the fire.
24 It requires an unshakable confidence in a higher purpose
25 than our own if we are to see victory for the Kingdom of
26 God. Let us all be reminded that the victory is not personally
27 for us but rather for the Kingdom.
28
29   People who *feel* their way through a relationship with
30 God also tend to read the Bible the same way. They read a
31 passage of Scripture and meditate waiting to see how it
32 makes them feel. They accept the "feeling" as though it is
33 the voice of God. These individuals are easily manipulated
34 and are highly susceptible to Satan's snares. Knowing how
35 to study Scripture correctly is the right place to start. Read it
36 in context. Understand the history behind the text. Know the

1 original meanings of the words in print. Meditate upon those
2 things and get a clear understanding of the presentation of
3 the text before concluding any specific message. Know that
4 Scripture doesn't exist to provide some secret personal
5 interpretation. It is written so that we may know Him better
6 and understand His character. It provides a guide for us and
7 establishes a base line of normality for us all. Hearing God
8 speak is awesome but that alone cannot be trusted if we do
9 not know the meaning of Scripture in its original context.
10 Voices in our head must never replace the written Word of
11 God. If it does, we will believe anything simply because it
12 popped into our heads. That makes it very easy for Satan to
13 get us off course. There is a movement today to devalue the
14 written Word and the reason is clear. People can say "God
15 told me" all they want to but if the Word doesn't confirm that
16 in context and precept, it's a lie from the enemy. Because
17 they are strategically duped, havoc ensues. This is all too
18 often the case with hyper-sensitive believers. They easily
19 buy into books that claim to be Jesus speaking but in reality
20 it is only human logic making a foolish attempt to suppose
21 God's thoughts. It is man's folly and it's dangerous. Our
22 feelings can and will change but God's Word remains the
23 same no matter the culture, the mood or the times. When I
24 hear people talking about "sensing" and "feeling"
25 something, my first inclination is to ask, what does God's
26 Word say? Our feelings will change but His Word never
27 changes. First know the truth and then have feelings about
28 it, not the other way around. This is how Satan manipulates
29 doctrines and cultural philosophies. He promotes
30 independent thinking apart from the Scriptures, makes us
31 feel intelligent, advanced and superior for the purpose of
32 leading us from the truth of the Word. This is indeed a
33 dangerous path. We mock God when we stand in defiance of
34 His Word. It is a certainty that God will indeed have the last
35 word. Satan's tricks undermine our divine assignment and
36 stop us cold in our tracks.

Soldiers who are in battle realize that the easiest thing they can do is to hide behind something to protect themselves but they know there is a bigger picture, a greater purpose that drives them to forge ahead even at their own peril. Where are these heroes of the faith? Where are these who are willing to boldly face the congregation that wants permission to depart from the Bible? Where are the pastors and leaders that will stand against the flow of popular opinion and fight the good fight of faith? I believe they are among us. I also believe that God is now raising them out of their obscurity for these last days. The days ahead will be of biblical proportions and we will be right in the middle of it all! God will have His way before it is all finished. Where will we stand in all of this? In large part, we can find the answer to that question in our resolve. How determined are we to see God's purposes fulfilled?

We will not be a part of His amazing plans if we don't get out of our immature mode of operation. God is not some alien who communicates by Morse code. He doesn't have a communication problem. He is not inept or incapable of speaking to us no matter how thick-headed we might be. He isn't pouting because we don't get it. He is proactively working to complete this interstellar project and He will do so right on time. Seeing beyond our foolish spiritism is necessary so that we may recognize His big picture. Spiritual obedience has more to do with seeking His will rather than our own. If we reject being overwhelmed by our little picture worlds, we might see things differently. Even though we often struggle with "what is God saying?" we could simply read the Bible to know what He says and **do that**. If we won't do what the Bible says then why do we think He's going to speak to us in our heads? Maybe if we meditate more, that might do it! This is a trick! Satan has duped a modern Christian world into believing that we should somehow become super spiritual without using the Bible as

1   our standard. Fasting, praying and meditation should be a
2   staple in every believer's life but it should **never** replace
3   studying His very Words. After all, what good is it to get the
4   flesh to empty itself of its will and have nothing to put into
5   it? This reminds me of the house that was swept clean but
6   nothing was put in its place. The demon returned with 7
7   others more evil than the first. We must have the Word in our
8   hearts or we will find our spirits compromised with
9   worldliness and phony-baloney hyper-spiritualism. Without
10 that, we are mere New Agers with no true source or root for
11 our faith. This ruse is a clever ploy and it is sad that it has
12 been so effective. Some people claim to be super spiritual
13 while at the same time they live with one to whom they are
14 not married. That's a direct violation of the Scriptures. I'm
15 not buying it. True godly spirituality embraces the Word and
16 never supersedes it. Some believe that the Word is outdated
17 for our times. The Word *IS* Jesus and He never changes (John
18 1). If we have changed so much that the Word is no longer
19 valid, **we have changed too much!** We must get back to the
20 Bible. When we do, God will speak.
21
22   The thing that Satan fears most is our potential to
23 become what God intended for us to be. If he can dupe us
24 and get us caught up in our little worlds then he cares little
25 about anything else. He knows that if our focus is on our
26 current circumstances then our future is of no consequence.
27 He does this to get us off of our assignments and into a
28 *malaise* of wandering and wondering. We will *always* have
29 trouble. When will we decide to ***persevere*** through it and get
30 on with the work of the Lord? When will we decide that we
31 have had enough distractions? When will we decide to get
32 our focus on the larger picture and realize that all we need to
33 do is surrender it all to the Lord? If we do, He will prove He
34 is powerful above all others! This is the system that He
35 created for us to successfully navigate the troubles of this

1   life. If we do not operate the system that He created, we will
2   get that which we deserve, a mess!
3
4   God does speak to us in a myriad of ways but be sure
5   what you hear is really God. The way you know that is to
6   balance it against the written Word. He never supersedes His
7   Word. Land in the Word **then** when you hear His voice, you
8   will recognize it. It won't be an act of superstition but rather,
9   an act of submission. Try the spirits to be sure they are of
10 God (I John 4:1). We should deeply desire to be spiritual but
11 its basis must be the written Word. When that is true we are
12 safe and more able to hear His voice. He will speak. The
13 question is, are we able to hear? When we hear something,
14 are we hearing Him or is it our own will telling us what to
15 do? To know the difference, we must know the Word.

Chapter 7
Superstition (more tricks)

Key Word Studies in Context

1. <u>Superstition</u> – (Pg. 77, #2), an irrational belief that an object, action, or circumstance not logically related to a course of events or thing, influences its outcome, disassociated from the actual truths of God.

2. <u>Nuance</u> – (Pg. 77, #9), a subtle but meaningful expression or a small difference in color, tone or shade, a subtle mood change in a meaning, a feeling.

3. <u>Incremental</u> – (Pg. 77, #9), small changes one at a time, slow orderly movement, step by step.

4. <u>Replete</u> – (Pg. 78, #27), abundantly supplied, filled.

5. <u>Malaise</u> – (Pg. 83, #28), feeling tired, detached, under the weather, lethargic.

6. <u>Persevere</u> – (Pg. 83, #29), to persist, endure, hold on through difficulty.

Workbook Activities

1. God is not silly and He has no problem communicating that which He wants us to know. Discuss the methods by which God speaks. How can we be sure that the voice we hear is actually the Holy Spirit speaking and not our own conscience? (Pg. 77, #4-35)

2. There is an inherent danger in thinking God is secretly trying to communicate with us in every detail in life. We can over-spiritualize things and become obsessive and paranoid in the process. Explain why this is dangerous and what can we do to avoid this errant behavior.
(Pg. 78, #1-36; Pg. 79, #1-7)

3. What is the danger of allowing circumstances to dictate God's will? (Pg. 79, #9-36; Pg. 80, #1-27)

4. Why are feelings alone not to be trusted?
(Pg. 80, #29-36; Pg. 81, #1-36)

5. What does having a made up mind have to do with success in battle? (Pg. 82, #1-16)

6. Believers are recommended to meditation upon His Word. What is the danger of just meditating without focusing upon the Word? (Pg. 82, #18-36; Pg. 83, #1-20)

7. How is Satan's ploy a diversion from our assignments? (Pg. 83, #22-35; Pg. 84, #1-15)

Chapter 8
The Pursuing

Most people mistakenly think that the "Assignment" is one big specific thing that we do such as an end goal. We have a tendency to believe that preaching or being some celebrity icon is the mark of ministerial success. We like to believe that we need to be a "Moses" of the Bible to be significant in this world of assignments. I believe this is contrary to the way God thinks. God seems to think in terms of what He wants for us to do in order to complete His plan. It rarely if ever has anything to do with us in terms of fame and popularity. In other words, He's not trying to make us rich and famous simply because He gives us a really *special* calling designed just for us. His assignments are plenteous and always based on that which He wants done. If we do become rich and famous, the intended goal is nevertheless for His glory and not our own.

Carnal thinking gets us into trouble constantly. God doesn't play that game. His thinking is much higher than ours. He sees the big picture and knows what we must do to affect tomorrow. It would be foolish of me to think that my only assignment is preaching or counseling. Sometimes my assignment is as simple as speaking a kind word or encouraging someone as they go along. What good is it to preach on the streets and brilliantly argue the case of Christ but then throw your hands up at someone at a stop sign because they are not moving as quickly as you think they should? Ministry has as much to do with the change and attitude of the heart as it does with the physical aspects of going out and boldly declaring the truths of God. I have found that whenever I feel His anointing to do something specific then that is my assignment. The Holy Spirit's goal is to glorify the Father just as Jesus did when He was upon

1 the earth. His purpose is not to glorify us. We have that
2 backward. Sometimes we get the cart before the horse and
3 think ministry is about us, thinking that bigger is always
4 better. The idea that only *big* ministry is meaningful to God
5 is foolish and it does not have a rightful place in our thinking
6 today. We also tend to think in terms of rank and **prestige**
7 when it comes to ministries. Our default thinking is that the
8 church cleaning lady is not as important as the pastor. Yes,
9 there are rules of order and the assertion for respect and
10 honor of specific leadership positions are clear in the Apostle
11 Paul's writings. He recommends double honor to those that
12 handle God's Word. However God tends to rank us
13 differently than we do. He speaks of the humble being
14 exalted and the meek inheriting the earth. He even made a
15 remark about the widow's mite that challenged the
16 Pharisees' perception of giving. So we must give up the idea
17 that the only important ministry is a pulpit ministry or the
18 ministry that has risen to stardom. It just has no merit in
19 God's world simply because of a title alone. While the Word
20 says to seek the best gifts, we should know that gifts are not
21 for *our* glory but rather for the greater good of the Kingdom
22 of God. If we do gain advantage by having a title, its
23 intended purpose is to exalt and promote the Kingdom of
24 God and not ourselves. We must never lose sight of the fact
25 that we are *servants* that work and maintain the Father's
26 business and not our own.
27
28 If we understand that God has called us to *something*,
29 what does it matter if we sweep a floor in abject obscurity or
30 if we stand in front of thousands of people singing His
31 praises? God doesn't measure success in the same way that
32 we do. What He wants is someone that will go and do as
33 instructed. He looks for someone whose mind is on Him and
34 not themselves. What difference does it make of how famous
35 we become from God's perspective? If it has no Kingdom
36 advantage, obviously it is of no use to the Kingdom. God

1   may just want the floor swept. He has His reasons. He
2   rewards obedience in a different way than we measure
3   success. What about the guy who simply cleans the church
4   with a heart of worship? It needs doing so that others may
5   have a place that is clean and prepared for their worship to
6   God. The quiet custodian that does this may be far more
7   spiritual than someone who is ***ego-centric*** and is the center
8   of attention. God looks at the heart and therefore, our
9   motives. Which of these examples would you think gives
10 God the most credit; a man who worships with his heart and
11 his broom or someone who hopes to be more famous with
12 every sermon preached? When stated that way, the answer is
13 obvious. The point is we should never underestimate our
14 assignment. We have no idea of the potential it holds to affect
15 the Kingdom of God since our view is so limited. In fact, we
16 should not look at assignments that way at all. We should
17 simply obey. Just do it and leave the rest to the Lord. He
18 knows how to raise us and He knows how to lower us. He
19 will not compete for glory. If we try to take His glory, we
20 invariably find ourselves in a state of confusion. The reason
21 for this is that the intended process for our assignment is not
22 for our glory at all. ALL glory goes to Him. So what does it
23 matter if we are famous or not? Who cares if people never
24 know our names? It's not about us at any level. It just isn't!
25 God can raise us up and if He does, it is always ultimately
26 for His purposes and not our own. We should be humbled by
27 anything God does with our name attached to it first by
28 remembering that we are all replaceable and unnecessary.
29 All that He does in regards to us is an act of grace. Another
30 thing to remember is that *He doesn't need us at all*. He's not
31 impressed with our degrees or skills in the slightest. All He
32 wants is for us to obey His voice and act accordingly. Yes,
33 there are many benefits to obedience but that's another book.
34
35   Living as though we are servants to His cause is a
36 true test of leadership. We must be good followers in order

1 to be good leaders. Are we following His voice, His biblical
2 order and His direction? Success is best measured by our
3 popularity with God rather than our popularity with man. So
4 drive the bus, sweep the floors, teach the children and preach
5 if you must. This in no way demeans the order or respect
6 afforded to those who handle the Word. They are worthy of
7 double honor but never let us become arrogant because of it.
8 If anything, preaching and teaching should be a humbling
9 experience. Just think of it, God uses these as vessels for His
10 Word. Wow! That should bring every preacher and teacher
11 to their knees. It's an assignment. The privilege of serving
12 can be taken from any of us at any time if it so pleases the
13 Lord. His purposes are greater than ours. He is the planner
14 and we are his servants. Even Jesus said as He spoke with
15 His Father, "Not my will but thine be done." He yielded to
16 His Father completely, keeping no glory for Himself. We
17 should learn from that.
18
19   Assignments are interesting because they really
20 don't start out with instructions per se. At least for us, they
21 begin with having a right attitude. To activate our
22 assignments, we must start with the right spirit and attitude
23 of heart. We can never fully experience the value and
24 purpose of the assignment otherwise. We might find
25 ourselves dancing around it for years but without the right
26 spirit, we will never fully accomplish it. Keep in mind that
27 God doesn't need us, ever! If we won't do it His way,
28 someone else will. It is a privilege to serve the King and the
29 rewards are out of this world!
30
31   The weightier matter may be more about assuming
32 the right attitude than about doing something that we
33 perceive to be monumental. In fact, we will find that the
34 "assignment" is more about having a long running series of
35 successful small assignments rather than an ultimate big
36 assignment. For example, someone might think that

1   preaching in front of millions of people is a big assignment.
2   Godly preachers who reach this mark do not get there in one
3   fell swoop. They get there as a result of a lifetime of ongoing
4   successful small assignments. However, we should not make
5   the mistake of assuming that preaching before millions is the
6   destination. We should nevertheless know that having the
7   right spirit in countless challenging settings does ready us
8   for a larger task. Again, the task itself is not our specific goal
9   but rather, growing in the Lord as we obey His instruction is
10   more needful for us.
11
12   Assignments are great training tools. They teach us
13   that we must maintain a humble and spiritual attitude no
14   matter what we go through. If we are servants of the Lord
15   then why assume abuse is personal? Why wouldn't we put
16   others above ourselves thinking that to be a normal spiritual
17   order? If we walk through the abuse while maintaining the
18   right spirit, we demonstrate that we have matured enough to
19   move to a new assignment. Never underestimate the power
20   of the assignment even if it is as simple as holding a door for
21   someone else. I know that sounds trivial but it demonstrates
22   that you respect that person and prefer them above yourself.
23   Isn't that the epitome of humility? Having a servants heart
24   enables us to walk in our assignments; moving from one to
25   another with relative ease. It is not about us becoming some
26   kind of spiritual giant as some may suppose. It is more about
27   us doing what He needs done to finish His work here on
28   earth. We have to learn how to do that by exercising our
29   assignment muscles. Adding understanding about an
30   assignment gives it meaning in our lives but is not necessary
31   to our accomplishing His orders. We don't have to know the
32   reasons for the orders that we receive. We simply have to
33   obey as good soldiers. Sometimes He gives us clarity and
34   that's awesome but that's His ***prerogative***. We are soldiers
35   in constant training, always learning a new procedure and
36   method of service. This broadens the effect of the Kingdom

of God. It starts and ends as a matter of the heart. **We must maintain the attitude of knowing that we are not necessary. It is a privilege to serve Christ.** We are replaceable at the drop of a hat and without Him we can do NOTHING, "I am the vine, ye are the branches: He that abideth in me, and I in him, the same bringeth forth much fruit: for without me ye can do nothing". (John 15:5). When we do His work, in essence we invade the darkness with His light!

Many people just give up because they measure assignments the way the world measures success. They think, "I could never be a preacher so why try." First of all, being a preacher is not as glorious as many think. People perceive the role as fun because Sunday's are entertaining and the preacher is funny or whatever. They are unaware of the constant complaining by some members, childish displays of emotions and constant fights over territory. These things should not exist but they do. Most pastors find themselves in a quandary. They feel the powerful persuasion of the Holy Spirit to build the Kingdom of God but instead they are relegated to the duties of a referee. He spends most of his time pulling people off of each other because of their fighting. It is indeed shameful and in no way reflects the church of the Bible. Sadly, we have become silly and as such we have missed our assignments on this earth. Further, the pastor is on call day and night. He cannot take a real vacation because the phone is always there and always ringing. He is a counselor, teacher, lawyer, defender, doctor, prayer, marketing expert, well dressed, genius and of course, perfect! IMPOSSIBLE! Here are some things that every pastor should know about the assignment of that role. Note: this isn't for the inexperienced or the faint of heart.

- Go in expecting it to be tough. Being naive will kill you.

- Don't go in with personal emotional baggage. They will discover it and beat you to death with it. Get it fixed first.
- Have the heart of Jesus. You're going to need it.
- Hold others in high esteem and cherish each of your leaders.
- Deeply love your congregation and don't let them go to sleep. Train them to do ministry no matter how new or old they are in the Lord.
- Expect challenges. These are humans. It's normal.
- Enjoy what you do. There are only a few out there that can do it. These skill sets are painful to come by.
- Keep your focus on Jesus and the assignment that He has given you. You can do it.
- You must fast, pray and study the Word constantly.
- Never believe you are irreplaceable. You're not.
- Do not neglect your family. Be PRESENT with them. Be deliberate about spending time with them.
- Do not have an illicit relationship with the church. She's someone else's bride. We are her caretakers until her bridegroom returns, nothing more. Fall in love with Jesus and build the Kingdom. He said "HE" would build His church.
- Pursue Him with every ounce of your being! The more you do, the more you want to. It is an awesome experience that is pure and full of love.
- Be at peace with your assignment. Don't "gold-dig", always being in search of something else. Be present in this assignment and let God alone deal with your future. Who knows, he may want to *elevate* you to become a broom pusher. Remember, it's always about the attitude of the heart.

Pursuing the assignment is really quite simple. Again, we must recognize that the assignment is not the only

1   goal. Establishing a right attitude about what we are going
2   through *at the time* is ALWAYS a large part of the goal. If
3   we do that, we never have to concern ourselves with the
4   results. We need only to maintain the right spirit through it
5   all. This is critically important to understand. Many people
6   search for a lifetime trying to figure out what they are
7   supposed to do but can't grasp the simple assignment of
8   opening a door for someone else. That is because we think
9   the assignment is some sort of landing place rather than
10 being part of the journey. Jesus along with others, including
11 the Apostle Paul knew that *the journey itself was the*
12 *assignment*. It was the day to day grind that seemed
13 inconsequential at the moment that they understood to be
14 their true purpose. It is easy to miss it. The truth is that the
15 total assignment is a **conglomeration** of mini-assignments.
16 Did you get that? Each opportunity to endure well gives us
17 purpose and fulfillment. Jesus explained that we are to
18 rejoice when men revile us and say all manner of evil against
19 us (Luke 6:23). Do you think that He was giving us a clue
20 on how to handle daily events in life? Clearly He was
21 addressing the attitude of the heart and as such He addressed
22 how to grasp our incremental assignments of life.
23
24   Always count it a privilege to serve no matter what
25 the assignment. The sad thing is we often miss it because we
26 willfully engage our emotions and then they take over and
27 dangerously guide us through everything. They take over the
28 helm as though they have the right to control our lives. This
29 usually ends in a total shipwreck. Emotions cannot grasp the
30 assignments of God because they don't always make sense
31 to us.
32
33   The flesh cannot discern things that are spiritual,
34 plain and simple, "But the natural man receiveth not the
35 things of the Spirit of God: for they are foolishness unto him:
36 neither can he know them, because they are spiritually

1   discerned." (I Corinthians 2:14). Our emotions want to pet
2   and protect us from every challenge in life. They can be so
3   powerful that they become our barometer, informing us of
4   its own interpretation as to what God "means" by all of this.
5   Because of this, we can become silly and superstitious in
6   regards to the meaning behind all that we go through. The
7   truth is it can be quite entertaining once you learn to stand
8   off to the side and recognize how crafty our emotions are.
9   They are self-preserving and they tend to betray the
10   assignment of God in the interest self-comfort; that is until
11   we forcefully remove them from power. Self-preservation is
12   what disrupts the assignment that God sends our way. It is
13   imperative that we see it for what it is. It seeks to please itself
14   and places God's purposes as a second or third place
15   possibility. You can see this today by examining the way
16   people attend church. They go to church nowadays only if
17   they have nothing else to do. Church no longer is a priority
18   because their hearts are far from Him. It's all about "family"
19   and "pleasure." Granted, we should love our families and we
20   should not feel guilty for taking a vacation but it is the
21   attitude of heart that I address. Many believe that as long as
22   they don't have something that they would rather do, they
23   then decide to go to church as though they are doing God a
24   favor. It really would be laughable if it weren't just so sad
25   because it is blatantly obvious that they do not understand
26   the need for being equipped and learning the Word of God.
27   Church is supposed to be an equipping center, preparing us
28   for service, not a clubhouse! Perhaps that's part of the
29   problem.
30
31   Most people see church in an errant perspective. The
32   intended purpose of the church is not to be a civic center or
33   a family reunion every Sunday although it is certainly
34   wonderful to get together. I would never diminish the
35   benefits of coming together but we should go to church with
36   the understanding that it is a training ground to do spiritual

battle. Keep in mind that church is not our destination but rather it is a place where we go for service training and to collectively worship the King as a body of believers. If it isn't, it should be. The very idea that church is a place to *land* as though it is the end goal is silly and anti-biblical. It is not supposed to be a secret society. It is a training center where people learn the Word of God and experience the effervescent flow of God's power. *It affirms and sends.* What good is the Gospel if it isn't preached to the lost? We spend so much time with our own psychological issues and emotional baggage that we miss our purpose. We use church for a mental health petting zoo instead of it being a place for mental and emotional healing. Get healed! Get equipped and go! Yes, counseling is in order sometimes but we need to get well and move on? The design of the church is not to be a **sanitarium** with permanent residency. Are we actively dealing with our own baggage with an expected result or do we simply cope with it and then wonder why we are not at peace? Satan is clever and uses our weaknesses against us. Let us address the root issues that hinder us and get on with the real reason we are here. **Strongholds** are Satan's favorite method of squandering our purposes on this earth. What a trickster! We are not subject to him. We can resist him and he will run in terror (James 4:7)! If need be, get the proper help needed and you too will see him flee in fear like a whimpering, defeated foe!

If we are so broken to the point that we cannot function, how can we help others or even pursue our assignments? First we have to recognize that *we are broken* and *need healing* for our own past, present and future. We need to be whole. Our collective need for repair is staggering. It isn't as though it is not available. It is. We just don't do it partly because we don't know that our baggage is killing our assignments. We think of them as normal and we accept them. Part of the pursuit of our assignments requires

1 that we prepare for service. That means that WE must go to
2 the altar where things die and we must connect with the
3 Almighty God for help. We must not coddle our damaged
4 emotions and assume that it is somehow acceptable and
5 normal. We owe this to the people that we influence. They
6 need to see how the Lord can heal brokenness. What we
7 typically see are people getting it backward by launching
8 into ministry without first looking in the mirror. We should
9 ask the Lord to search our hearts to see if there is any wicked
10 way in us or for that matter, any broken thing in us. If we
11 ignore this, it will rear its ugly head and be a powerful source
12 for discouragement in the future. Look for it and expect it
13 because Satan just cannot pass this up; it's that easy for him.
14
15   Understanding the *reason behind why we do ministry*
16 can often determine our ability to endure. Our assignments
17 should not be a sole response to what happened to us as
18 children but rather a pure and unadulterated rallying to the
19 call of God. Many serve because they still try to address their
20 own brokenness. While remembering the things that God
21 brought us through is acceptable and sometimes helpful, we
22 should never let those things be our sole reason for entering
23 ministry. It doesn't work. For example, some people treated
24 badly as children feel a need to help children. Is that the
25 result of a call or a response to an inner need? If we merely
26 respond to our *need* then the first time we feel rejection in
27 our ministry of helping kids, we want to quit because **pain**
28 **overtakes the calling**. However if we respond directly to our
29 call from God, no matter what comes against us, we are all
30 in and at the core equipped to persevere. Our emotions do
31 not take the lead but rather, we respond to the actual call of
32 God. God can use a ragged past to push us toward something
33 but we must not allow an experience (good or bad) to be
34 what calls us into ministry. Be sure to enter ministry because
35 He has called you and *then* He will add to that the benefit of
36 your experience as well. Let me reiterate this once again.

1   Responding to former pain as though it is a calling usually
2   results in a very short term ministry. Inconvenience and the
3   constant lack of ***affirmation*** can ruin a ministry when based
4   upon emotional needs. In other words, if we do ministry
5   based on the thinking that it is easy and people will love us
6   for it, we are in for a rude awakening. Ministry is rarely easy
7   as a whole. There are moments of appreciation but more
8   often than not, it is a lonely road surrounded by people who
9   just don't get it. That's the sad truth of it. That's why we
10   have to serve God because He called us to do something
11   rather than for the thrills we might get or for the emotional
12   affirmation that we secretly need. Really think about that.
13   We should get our affirmation from Him and not try to work
14   a ministry so that it will fix our bad imprints or pain from the
15   past. It just doesn't work. Most people are unwilling to
16   endure the pain that goes with ministry. This is often why
17   people quit in mid-stream.
18
19   If the root of why we do ministry is not pure, the fruit
20   of it won't be pure either. We tend to reproduce "after our
21   own kind." Broken begets broken. Jesus came to fix the
22   broken. Get fixed first by falling in love with Him and letting
23   Him do the emotional surgery in you and **then** pursue
24   ministry. We are called to it. If you are engaged in ministry
25   and discover that your original motives may not be as pure
26   as you wish, take it to Jesus. He knows exactly what to do.
27   He can fix us even if we are already in the process of leading
28   others. It's a good thing that He can! We need it! One thing
29   is certain; if you do fall in this category, your life is about to
30   radically change. Your thinking is about to be transformed
31   and your purposes will soon become dramatically different!
32   Ministry will take on a whole new persona and you will
33   finally find the peace for which you have searched so long.
34   The journey is worth it! The Kingdom is better for it as well.
35   Having a pure motive assures us that God will bless it and
36   accomplish that which He alone can do. Part of your journey

1   may include seeing a godly counselor. Good; then do it!
2   They often can give you the skills to navigate common
3   scenarios along with those negative, pervasive and dominant
4   thinking processes. Freedom from these is often surprisingly
5   more powerful than many can imagine. Start at the altar of
6   God and seek Him. If God places a real counselor in your
7   life, that's great but just do it no matter what it takes! The
8   effects are far reaching and in fact, immeasurable!

Chapter 8
The Pursuing

Key Study Words in Context

1. <u>Carnal</u> – (Pg. 88, #20), in religious terms, fleshly, as directed by human thinking, worldly or humanistic in nature, devoid of godly influence.

2. <u>Prestige</u> – (Pg. 89, #6), a high standing based on the perceptions of others.

3. <u>Ego-centric</u> – (Pg. 90, #7), self-centered, about one's self.

4. <u>Prerogative</u> – (Pg. 92, #34), the right to a decision.

5. <u>Elevate</u> – (Pg. 94, #30), to lift up, exalt, to push upward.

6. <u>Conglomeration</u> – (Pg. 95, #15), a grouping of things, a group made up of many companies or entities.

7. <u>Sanitarium</u> – (Pg. 97, #16), a healing place for the mentally ill.

8. <u>Strongholds</u> – (Pg. 97, #21), chains, barriers, weapons of intimidation, reasons we give for failure.

9. <u>Affirmation</u> – (Pg. 99, #3), positive words that lift up and encourage, the act of being approved.

The Pursuing

Workbook Activities

1. Is our assignment one big thing that we do or is it a series of mini-assignments along the way? Explain your answer. (Pg. 88, #4-18)

2. How does God measure spiritual success and how does that compare with the secular perspective? (Pg. 88, #20-35; Pg. 89, #1-26)

3. Our assignments have a specific purpose and design. What do you think that is? (Pg. 89, #28-36; Pg. 90, #1-33)

4. Why is it necessary to be good followers before we can be good leaders? (Pg. 90, #35-36; Pg. 91, #1-17)

5. God doesn't "need" us to fulfill His plans. Why is this? (Pg. 91, #19-29)

6. Is the assignment the destination or part of the journey? (Pg. 91, #31-36; Pg. 92, #1-10)

7. What is the true measure and value of an assignment? Who decides this? (Pg. 92, #12-36; Pg. 93, #1-9)

8. Name some burdens that pastors often face. (Pg. 93, #11-33)

9. Discuss the kind of thinking needed for the purpose of successfully operating ministry. (Pg. 93, #35-36; Pg. 94, #1-32)

10. The assignment must not be a landing place. Why is this? (Pg. 94, #34-35; Pg. 95, #1-22)

11. How can our emotions challenge our ability to do our assignments? (Pg. 95, #24-31)

12. The personal healing of our emotional baggage is imperative so that we can touch others with the Gospel of Jesus. Discuss this in detail.
(Pg. 95, #33-36; Pg. 96, #1-29)

13. The collective church body is desperate for emotional healing. Why do we need to address this?
(Pg. 96, #31-36; Pg. 97, #1-26)

14. Why do we need to understand the real motive for our ministry interests? (Pg. 97, #28-36; Pg. 98, #1-13)

15. Being at peace with God AND with one's self is of a great benefit to the each of us as we touch others for Jesus. Explain the reasons and the benefits.
(Pg. 98, #15-36; Pg. 99, #1-17)

16. Why is it so important for our motives to be pure as we pursue our assignments? (Pg. 99, #19-36; Pg. 100, #1-8)

Chapter 9
Divine *Persuasion*

For many years I had heard a lot of preachers particularly in charismatic circles, speak of how to increase one's faith. Their premise seemed to be a matter of convincing the mind that God could do something. Their concept appeared to indicate that if we convinced ourselves enough that God **could** do something then He **would** do it simply based on the idea that we had come into agreement with Him. While there may be *some* elements of truth found in this concept, let us first go back to the root of the word "faith." According to Strong's Concordance, the word "faith" is best described as "God's Divine persuasion." Jesus asked His disciples, "How is it that you have no faith?" He was actually asking them why they hadn't picked up on God's "divine persuasion" especially since He was standing before them. Based on this, having faith is not an exercise in how many times we attempt to convince ourselves that God wants to do a particular thing. Repeating over and over that you believe does not change the fact that before faith can exist we have to have "God's divine persuasion." In other words, He is the one that initiates the process. He sets the assignment into motion. Simply saying, "I think I can" 500 times does not constitute having faith. Neither does such behavior alter God's thinking. True faith is simply responding to the assignment that He has just spoken to you. He will *divinely persuade* you to the point that you KNOW what to do. Granted, He may not always give the full picture but He will give you enough to get you started for that moment. When it comes time for more, it will be there. Can we improve on hearing God's Divine persuasion? Sure we can! But we do not have faith simply by forcing our minds to agree with Him alone. Before Jesus did miracles, He conferred with His Father (John 5:19, 30). He did nothing of

His own and the very idea that we can is rooted in heresy. We operate solely by His instruction. He sends the assignment and we simply obey. The idea that we can conger up something that isn't there is foolish.

Having faith is really much simpler than many think. If we wait upon the Lord, He will tell us what to do. He will "persuade" us to do that which He asks. This is the essence of the assignment. Without His involvement, we only operate in the flesh. Apart from His influence, we can speak all we want to; it's not God speaking. Jesus repeated over and over that He did not come to do His own will but rather He came to do the will of His Father. He awaited His Father's instruction before He moved forward. He clearly indicated that the entire process was not about Him; it was about His Father. The modern **hyper-charismatic**, hyper-spiritual culture has skewed that perspective to the point that they have become more interested in wealth and self-preservation than about the will of God. The philosophy that *if I can believe it then I can have it* does not have its roots in the Word but instead, in the world. This is not to say that God can't or won't bless His people. He can and He does bless them quite often. We should realize that these blessings are for advancing **His** purposes and not necessarily our own. God has already put into place provision for His saints. Our instructions are first to seek the Kingdom of God, then we have access to the balance of blessings as He promised. We need not ask for that which has already been given. He provides us with "things" for the purpose of *perpetuating* the Kingdom of God. You see again, it's not about us after all.

Faith is a gift from God and all the intentional mental envisioning that one can muster won't do what the sovereign will of God can do. The fact is that our "ASSIGNMENT" is nothing more than God giving us our orders. It's not mysterious and fleeting as some might suppose.

1   Understanding the assignment is simply allowing God to
2   persuade us. He does this in many ways. We cannot speak to
3   the mountain and expect it to obey us if we are exercising
4   human desire alone. That's foolish. **If He gives us an**
5   **assignment** (a divine persuasion) ***THEN*** we can speak to the
6   mountain, cast it into the sea and it will obey us, not because
7   of our identities but His. The mountain does not recognize
8   my will but the force of nature absolutely MUST respond to
9   the will of its Creator. When we act on our own accord, we
10   are powerless but when we do His bidding, the mountain
11   must obey. Even if the persuasion is little and as small as a
12   grain of mustard seed, He will perform His will. No matter
13   how small the assignment, it still has the full force of God
14   when it originates from Him. In such a case, the small
15   mustard seed indicates a small assignment. Nevertheless, no
16   matter how small things appear to us, God has a purpose that
17   is very big. This concept removes the guilt process that most
18   people feel when they pray for the sick and they *do not*
19   recover. Is it a "divine persuasion" or not? Did God send you
20   on an assignment to heal Suzie of cancer or did He call you
21   to pray a prayer of comfort? If He sent you to heal her, then
22   it's not you that's doing the work anyway, right? He didn't
23   call us to heal everybody. If He did, the hospitals would be
24   empty and disease would cease to exist in our world today.
25   We somehow believe that God came to heal the whole world
26   or that the whole world will experience salvation but that is
27   not true. He came to save the lost but they can only be truly
28   born again ***IF*** the Holy Spirit draws them (John 15:16). It is
29   not we who do the drawing. Whoever it is that has the right
30   to salvation is a decision that is above our pay grades. One
31   thing is a certainty, when He sets the scene for salvation; it's
32   for a reason that **supersedes** any of our own ideas and
33   theories. One sows, another waters but God gives the
34   increase (I Corinthians 3:7). He knows what it takes to
35   complete a spiritual equation. We may be a small part of that
36   equation so it is ***imperative*** that we simply obey Him and

1 leave the results to Him. This way we cannot take the blame
2 or the credit for whatever occurs.
3
4   What are we to do if our assignment brings us
5 significant personal pain? There are some who might believe
6 that God has mistreated them as they experience a personal
7 difficulty or tragedy. First let me state that this and other
8 experiences like it can seem overwhelming. The question
9 remains, why would God allow such things to occur if He
10 truly loves us? This question indicates that our premise is
11 that we often believe that everything is about us. It isn't.
12 While we are an integral *part* of the plan of God, *we are not*
13 *the whole plan.* As "slaves" we are His servants but as "sons"
14 we are partakers of His reward. There are many factors to
15 His plan that even the best theologians don't begin to
16 understand. Living out our mission to this darkened and
17 wicked world is enough to shake our idea that this life
18 experience is only about having jobs, feeding our families
19 and going on our merry way. While those are some
20 wonderful benefits to living, the plan is bigger, WAY
21 BIGGER than that. Once we get that fact, it moves us more
22 toward the understanding that our reason to be here is to be
23 all about Him. The idea gets even more traction when we
24 realize that faith comes from God and not from our mental
25 abilities to believe. Believing is very important but the root
26 of faith must come from God. He gives the assignment and
27 we act upon it. Any action that we take outside of the
28 assignment that God gives is just us acting on our own.
29 Understanding the origins of our faith is critical to the actual
30 performance of our beliefs. In other words, it must come
31 from God and not originate within ourselves. If we don't
32 grasp this simple truth initially, we are destined to wander
33 confused through life until we do. Also, once we accept that
34 our assignment is in the middle of this war zone for the
35 purpose of reestablishing His Kingdom, the pain we endure
36 makes more sense. This perspective helps to establish a

clearer picture of our reason to be. It also removes the guilt factor when we can't perform miracles at will. We must do His work at His bidding.

God makes no attempt to be aloof or distant in any way concerning these matters. It seems clearer than ever that *we have* complicated the reason for our being on this planet. We built an entire society that has a spirit of self-exaltation to such a magnitude that we **evade** the obvious. We have muddied the waters to the extent that for most of us, life remains a mystery. That is not at all God's plan. He is quite clear about His intentions for us but we spend most of our time trying to reconcile what *He requires* with that which *we want*. Do you also see a problem here? Learning to walk in His "Divine Persuasion" is the key. Look for the faith that He establishes in you. That's your assignment. Live by it and be faithful to it. Do not veer from it. Stay the course and do His bidding. It is imperative to our joy and our peace to follow the path that He has for us. If we won't do it, He will raise up another to fulfill His will on this earth. He doesn't need us; we need Him.

Chapter 9
Divine Persuasion

Key Study Words in Context

1. <u>Persuasion</u> – (Pg. 105, #2), convincing others or causing someone to change their mind.

2. <u>Hyper-charismatic</u> – (Pg. 106, #16), overly emphasizing the works of the Holy Spirit in comparison with Acts 2, developing an unbiblical and emotional belief of supernatural effects outside of biblical context, e.g., people barking like dogs, gold dust falling from the sky, feathers falling from the air, hearing God when He's not speaking and believing one has the power to speak things into existence apart from the specific command of God to do so.

3. <u>Perpetuating</u> – (Pg. 106, #29), to cause to continue, the act of deliberately promoting existing motion.

4. <u>Supersedes</u> – (Pg. 107, #32), goes above, to the take the place of something.

5. <u>Imperative</u> – (Pg. 107, #36), very important, an expression of something urgent or necessary.

6. <u>Evade</u> – (Pg. 109, #9), to stay away from, avoid, go the other way.

Workbook Activities

1. What is the biblical meaning for the word "faith"?
   (Page 105, #4-35; Page 106, #1-4)

2. Because faith comes from God and since His instructions
   are our assignments, how does this affect the way we
   think about our purpose here on earth? (Pg. 106, #6-30)

3. What is the relationship between "faith", "divine
   persuasion" and assignments?
   (Pg. 106, #32-36; Pg. 107, #1-36; Pg. 108, #1-2)

4. How does understanding the origin of faith help us to
   endure pain better? (Pg. 108, #4-36; Pg. 109, #1-3)

5. God's voice is clear. He does not have a communication
   problem. He first speaks in His Word then He speaks to
   our spirit. We get that backward most of the time.
   Discuss why that is and what happens when we do. How
   can we fix that? (Pg. 109, #5-21)

Chapter 10
Entanglement

One of Satan's highest and most preferred tools is what I call "entanglement." He has an amazing knack for turning small things into big things. He promotes panic and anxiety constantly. Because of this, we apparently adjust to his game rather than forcing him to adjust to God's plan. He does this with ease simply because we are unaware of the terms of war. God set the rules of engagement but they have no force unless we assert them.

The art of entanglement is fascinating. It is really nothing more than placing a proverbial magnifying glass on any given subject. Entanglement is a trick that consists of an overemphasis of a potential problem. The ploy is to get us to believe that whatever is before us is the most important thing in the world. It blows up everything and makes it appear to be critical when reality is in a hundred years it won't matter.

If Satan can trick us into believing that we are the reason the world exists then there is a high likelihood that we will live that way in practice. When something goes wrong in life, we automatically assume it's because we've been bad or God doesn't love us. Satan deliberately feeds our egos and convinces us that we are the center of the universe so when bad things happen we take it as a direct, personal assault and then accuse God of not loving us. I mentioned earlier, we should remember that we've been deployed into an active war zone to assert God's authority and to establish His Kingdom on earth. Satan's attempt to entangle us deeply in our own affairs has a specific dark logic to it. Clearly his efforts aren't solely for the purpose of merely irritating us. His plan is much more sinister. He intends to preoccupy us with our own affairs to the point that

1   we ignore the more weighty matters of our true purposes.
2   Basically he gets us off course and preoccupies us for a
3   lifetime. We believe this to be normal since this is all we
4   have known. We call it "life" although that's not really living
5   at all. There is no doubt that Satan laughs at our **gullibility**.
6   Our problem is that we believe that the entire universe is
7   about us and the total plan of God is all about us; it's not.
8   We have bought a bill of goods that has compromised our
9   very reason to be. This is a tragic fallacy. Take a look at II
10   Timothy 2:3-4. "Thou therefore endure hardness, as a good
11   soldier of Jesus Christ. No man that warreth entangleth
12   himself with the affairs of this life; that he may please him
13   who hath chosen him to be a soldier."
14

15   Some years ago, the famous radio personality Paul
16   Harvey wrote a candid and startling commentary called "If I
17   were the Devil." He proceeded to write about the methods
18   that Satan would use to corrupt America and the modern
19   Christian church. It is frightening to listen to even today
20   because his points are poignant and powerful particularly
21   since he wrote it decades ago. I would like to venture my
22   own version if I may. Notice Satan's attempt to entangle us.
23

24   If I were the Devil …
25   •   I would arrange it so that Christians felt that they
26   were disfavored and thought of as bigots and
27   intolerant. I would use this to further intimidate them
28   and get them to shut their mouths.
29   •   I would encourage them to be so busy that they
30   would not have time to focus on anything other than
31   their own little worlds.
32   •   I would create a setting where they would think of
33   Christianity as an **addition** to their already busy
34   lifestyle rather than actually *being* their lifestyle.

- I would lie to them about Jesus and tell them that He doesn't care about how they live and that He is okay with them no matter what their behavior.
- I would get them to worship their children but I would do it under the guise of preserving **posterity**.
- I would see that every believer became short sighted, unable to see the forest for the trees. They would not have a big picture for the long term or see the big plan of God. This would make them narrow focused. They would live for now and remove themselves from any concerns of the long term future.
- I would be sure they were addicted to pleasure. I would sell them a bill-of-goods of indulgence in order to ensure that they were all about themselves.
- I would make sure that church is merely a social club and a place where people come for affirmation and a feel-good experience.
- I would challenge them on gender, biblical truth and moral turpitude. I would tell them that God really doesn't care about such matters because He loves them the way they are. I would destroy the concept of conversion and replace it with the doctrine of false grace.
- I would teach them that repentance is simply being sorry for sinning rather than having a life change, supernaturally brought about by the Holy Spirit, assuring them that real conversion doesn't exist.
- I would tell them that spirituality is reserved for fanatics and religious addicts. I would let them think that being spiritual is weird and not normal.
- I would make sure that abusive people who call themselves Christians would be the standard by which the world judges Christianity.
- I would use the phrase, "judge not" over and over again until they believe that they have no right to

assert biblical truth. This would nullify any biblical mandate to live holy.

- I would create a culture of avarice and greed inside the church. I would teach them that God is their butler and all we have to do is to speak it and He will obey. I would teach them that debt is okay since everybody has it.
- I would corrupt pulpits and tell them that the Bible is not really God's Word. I would assert that the words in the Bible were the opinions of men.
- I would convince them that drinking alcohol is normal and that substance addiction is something that only happens to *other* people.
- I would so water down the Gospel that people would not be able to tell the difference between the lifestyles of sinners and believers.
- I would make sure that pastors are mere hirelings and give all the church decision making power to spiritual infants.
- I would reduce the meaning behind sacred things and call them mere religious icons. I would decimate their religious history and nullify their heritage as meaningless.
- I would teach them that tithing is only an Old Testament teaching and has nothing to do with the modern church of today.
- I would keep them broke all of the time requiring them to be slaves to the lender; always paying someone else with their own labor.
- I would make them feel a surge of self-worth every time they bought a new car or bought a new stereo. I would make this their new addiction, trading their money for pleasure.

1   Obviously this list could go on and on. Without
2 question Satan is busy developing his culture of loss and pain
3 under the ***guise*** of success and wealth. At first it appears that
4 his methods offer unending goods and services but then it
5 comes time to pay the piper. The cost of paying homage to
6 his pernicious culture is staggering. What would happen if
7 we simply said "NO!" to his foolishness? What if we were
8 to reject his lies out-right, knowing that he only wishes to
9 kill, steal and destroy us? What would happen if we were to
10 catch him at his tricks and tell him to get out? We would find
11 a freedom like we have never experienced before. He would
12 no longer have the ability to overwhelm us in the
13 entanglements of this life. Jesus defeated all of Satan's antics
14 on the Cross. Why do we assume that it is necessary to swap
15 blows with him when Jesus took care of all that? It's a trick!
16 It is a fool's game. Some spend a lifetime believing it's their
17 job to fight the devil! It's never been our job to fight him.
18 We resist him by submitting ourselves to God. When we do
19 this, we move from self-reliance to reliance upon the power
20 of God. It then becomes God's business. Satan is no match
21 for God! Let us make up our minds not to become entangled
22 with things that won't matter in a hundred years. Jesus said,
23 "Take no thought for your life, what ye shall eat, what ye
24 shall put on… (Matthew 6:25)." Yet we see Satan putting
25 extreme emphasis on all those incidental things. They are
26 incidental to God because He automatically provides them.
27 Getting caught up in life's cares is a trick of the enemy. We
28 need the 100 year plan! We need to ***disallow*** things from
29 consuming us intentionally. We also need to take a proactive
30 stand and get on with the Father's business! We have stood
31 idle and been victims long enough. It's time to make a
32 change. If it won't matter in a hundred years, then it doesn't
33 matter.

Chapter 10
The 100 Year Plan vs Entanglement

Key Study Words in Context

1. Entanglement – (Pg. 112, #2), to be tangled up in something, caught in a snare, to be caught up in something.

2. Gullibility – (Pg. 113, #5), vulnerable to the point of being predictable in one's acceptance of a thing, over trusting, easy to persuade.

3. Posterity – (Pg. 114, #5), future generations, for the sake of the future.

4. Guise – (Pg. 116, # 3), not the true nature of something, concealing its true nature.

5. Disallow – (Pg. 116, #28), refuse to permit, to stop something.

Workbook Activities

1. What are some of the methods of Satan to entangle us in life? (Pg. 112, #4-11)

2. What would be the point of Satan overemphasizing certain things in life? (Pg. 112, #13-19)

3. Discuss the overall plan of God and determine why it is not all about us but rather about God.
(Pg. 112, #21-35; Pg. 113, #1-13)

4. Discuss some of Satan's modern tricks he employs today.
(Pg. 113, #15-34; Pg. 114, #1-35; Pg. 115, #1-33)

5. Some believe that their assignment is to fight Satan. Is that the truth? What is our real assignment?
(Pg. 116, #1-33)

Chapter 11
The Assignment of *Loss*

All of life's common **distractions** really do keep us from feeling fulfilled in life. Let me reassert here the value of the 100 year plan. If we take on that concept, we are much less likely to allow the folly of this life to sidetrack us. Understanding that our assignment is to serve well no matter what happens is a key to living a full and rich life. What would happen if your house burned down tonight? Do you have a grasp of your assignment enough to get through that? No one said it would be easy but having the big picture of God's purpose for your life does help to make sense of it all. There is nothing easy about loss. I am certainly not proposing that we won't feel pain simply by getting the 100 year plan concept. However I do suggest that **grieving** will not endure forever if we get our assignment and live on the 100 year plan. This idea gives us closure and the ability to move on but then we have to *want* to and be willing to make those choices.

Researchers believe that when someone loses a spouse to death, their grieving period runs on the average of 5 years. This doesn't mean that they don't miss them or that their loved one doesn't matter anymore but it does mean that they somehow have come to the emotional conclusion that they have to move on and live the life that God gave them. There are many factors to the grief process and I don't wish to oversimplify it but sooner or later, we have to make a proactive decision to live our lives and fulfill the purpose to which God has called us. Will we have pain? Yes we will but we are here on an assignment nevertheless. Eventually, we must get back in the game and not allow circumstances to interfere with our ultimate reason to be. Again, grieving is a process. It is different for each of us but making a conscious

1 decision to move on does not have to feel as though we have
2 abandoned our lost loved ones. Moving on can actually be a
3 tribute to them. Most of us would agree that the one that we
4 long for and grieve over would want us to move on and live
5 life fully. They would want us to carry on and fulfill our
6 *divine* purpose on earth since we are still here. So after the
7 initial pain of loss, hopefully we come to the place where we
8 feel we can best honor our friend, spouse or family member
9 by moving forward, continuing to bring salt and light to the
10 world for Christ's sake. Having a small picture causes us to
11 remain in our state of loss perhaps forever. A big picture
12 enables us to honor our losses by forging ahead and fulfilling
13 the purposes of God for our own lives. If this seems
14 insensitive to loss and personal pain, I don't mean for it to
15 be. I do know loss but I also know that it can eventually
16 cripple our purpose and limit us from fulfilling our destinies
17 to which God has us assigned. This too can be a tool of the
18 enemy.
19
20 Let me reiterate that the **grief we feel is just a**
21 **reminder that we will never forget a lost one**. Slow down
22 for a minute and read that line again. This is why people hold
23 on to grief so closely. It is the closest that they can get to
24 their loved one that has passed away from the earth. The
25 reason many hold grief so closely is often because they fear
26 that if they let it go it will somehow lessen the intensity of
27 their love. There will come a time when turning that grief
28 into something positive may be the best way to remember a
29 spouse, family member or a friend. Let grief run its normal
30 course. In the proper perspective, it is a healthy thing. We
31 tend to find comfort in the fact that we are determined not to
32 stop loving them by never forgetting them. Once this is
33 established, moving on to living life further enables and
34 deepens that respect and love. It is a tribute and an honor to
35 them for us to move forward and live life to its fullest. Let
36 me put it this way; we find more peace in these situations

1 when we learn to celebrate their lives more so than when we
2 mourn them. Perpetual mourning almost seems to forfeit the
3 joy of having them for the amount of time that we did. If we
4 spend all of our time mourning, where is the celebration for
5 the life they lived? It's a delicate balance but we must move
6 forward into the celebration mode thanking God that we had
7 the chance to spend time with such a remarkable individual.
8 What a gift! That's what we celebrate! This is not a betrayal
9 of them. The act of celebrating them serves as a continual
10 reminder that they meant something profound in our lives
11 and that they will never be forgotten. Mourning in perpetuity
12 leaves a wake of brokenness and pain. Who would want this
13 for those that remain? If anyone knows about assignments,
14 it's those who have entered into the presence of the Lord.
15 They know the full extent of how important it is for us to
16 work while we can. They also know that life is not about us
17 or about those who have gone before us. They know that it
18 is all about the Glory of God. So do we honor them by living
19 in perpetual mourning or should we accentuate their
20 influence more by celebrating their lives? After all, if they
21 were a light to those around them, then accentuating that
22 only perpetuates their influence by affirming the reason that
23 they lived, right? It seems more meaningful to do that than
24 to grieve forever and waste their beautiful life of influence
25 as well as our own.
26
27   There is nothing wrong or improper with going
28 through the grieving process. It's normal and it does help us
29 to have closure on *what was* and to move on to *what will be*.
30 That can be a difficult leap for some of us. Of course, the
31 process is not instantaneous. It is sometimes a slow
32 progression but it should nevertheless be our goal. Even
33 though loss can feel unbearable when coupling that with all
34 the other things that life throws at us, there is still hope in
35 Jesus! He has a plan for our lives, even in the midst of
36 tragedy. In fact, Jeremiah 29:11 states that "I know the plans

1 I have for you, to prosper you and not to harm you..." Are
2 we enduring well? Are we living on the 100 year plan? Are
3 we keeping our focus on the finish line rather than the sharp
4 and painful side-stitch we feel at the moment? Do we feel
5 pain in our legs and feet as we run the race? We always run
6 the race better if we focus on the finish line. It is there,
7 awaiting our eventual crossing. *We have a purpose through*
8 *it all and that is to bring the light of God to every situation*
9 *that we face; including loss.* Please stop and read that line
10 one more time. Whether life is tragic, difficult or even
11 unbearable, we must endure hardness as a good soldier. The
12 concept of the 100 year plan is a powerful tool to get us
13 through. It teaches us to be proactive rather than reactive.
14 That is a key to enduring well. It teaches us not to get
15 overwhelmed with our circumstances. Life will go on
16 tomorrow but we have to want to join it by refusing to let it
17 pass us by. Life is short. We don't get a second chance. Don't
18 let *real* life pass you by! It's there on the sideline, looking at
19 you awaiting your plan of action to engage it. The plan that
20 God has for your life is phenomenal! Don't stop! Go for it!

Chapter 11
The Assignment of Loss

Key Study Words in Context

1. <u>Loss</u> – (Pg. 119, #2), the act of losing something, deprivation, pain of missing something or someone that is loved and cherished.

2. <u>Distractions</u> – (Pg. 119, #4), something that defers attention, an intentional act of diverting one's thoughts.

3. <u>Grieving</u> – (Pg. 119#16), the feeling of deep sorrow or loss, often a healing period in which an individual gains self-assurance that they will never forget their loved one.

4. <u>Divine</u> – (Pg. 120, #6), a word from God, holy assignment, sent from God.

Workbook Activities

1. Discuss the reason that Christians are not exempt from pain and sorrow. What should our response be to challenges in life? (Pg. 119, #4-20)

2. What does having a big picture have to do with getting through loss? How can we feel assured that we are not abandoning our loved ones by moving on?
(Pg. 119, #22-35; Pg. 120, #1-18)

3. Why do we tend to hold on to grief so closely?
(Pg. 120, #20-36; Pg. 121, #1-25)

4. Why does it help to focus on the finish line?
(Pg. 121, #27-36; Pg. 122, #1-20)

Chapter 12
It's Right in Front of You

I often hear people express their desire to know the will of God for their lives. It is always wonderful to hear when people long to please the Lord. When it comes to doing ministry, most of us look for something specific such as a pulpit or a teaching role of some kind. We can miss the obvious by assuming a title provides all that we need. There is a verse of Scripture that is a constant reminder not to despise small beginnings. That passage is found in Zechariah 4:10. We are often so goal oriented that we tend to expect complete success instantaneously. When someone feels an urgency to find their place in the grand scheme of things, they begin their search to find something that satisfies their skill set in hopes of discovering the will of God.

Obviously, we do not begin with a pulpit. We begin with a personal assessment of where we are with God. We work on the person in the mirror. We work on personal baggage and things that interfere with the flow of the Holy Spirit in our own lives. It's easy to jump right into something with a ministry label because we are so goal driven. Preparation is a very important key. Even the disciples who traveled and ate with Jesus day after day didn't do much for most of their time together because they were still getting their training. They spent their time observing and learning about the true culture and nature of God. They all had their ideas but Jesus didn't call them for the purpose of accessing their own ideas and concepts; He called them to share the culture of His Father. They didn't lift a hand to do *"ministry"* until Jesus gave them their ministry assignment. Some things that occurred were clearly for their own personal learning but as they progressed, they began to be more able to see the heart of God for their own lives. Self-preparation is extremely important. This includes **self-examination**. Let's take a look at the normal line of progression in order for one to accomplish the will of God for his or her life.

- Look in the mirror. You're not ready to lead others until you diligently work on yourself. Have **self-discipline**. Get rid of bad habits and prove the power of God in your life to change not only the heart but to affect the human spirit as well. GROW in God.
- Fix the problems from the past and any hindrances that offend the Holy Spirit.
- Be an extreme prayer warrior. Fast often and stop the flesh from bossing your spirit-man around.
- Learn the art of submission to those over you in the Lord. There is something very sweet and safe about recognizing the covering of God. This is His plan for us. Our pictures can be small but those over us see a bigger picture and are privy to more information in a grander scheme.
- Stop thinking that ministry always has some kind of title to it before considering it to be the "work of the Lord." Do not underestimate the value of service even if you believe it is inconsequential. If God has called you to it, it is ALWAYS meaningful and substantial in His Kingdom no matter how we see it as humans.
- Gain influence by exhibiting true and sincere loyalty to the faith, your church covering and your leaders.
- Learn and glean and think more in terms of being a humble servant rather than the top leader.
- Be the best follower that you know.
- Genuinely appreciate the gifts that others exhibit and edify them.

- Come under the mentorship of others. Learn and be quiet for a while until God gives you a voice by way of the leadership that He has placed over you.
- As you are spiritually able, make friends with sinners and learn to gain influence with them.
- Learn to share your faith softly and patiently as well as boldly. There will be a need for all of these.
- Titles in ministry alone do not determine true ministerial value. A lifestyle of service is what makes ministry valuable.
- Begin by loving *deliberately*. Open the door for someone else. Smile and cause someone to feel important. Do random acts of kindness. Be light in the midst of darkness. All of this is important ministry. What good are we if we storm the heights with pulpits or upon religious soap boxes but we won't wave at our neighbor or speak to someone in the hallway? I Corinthians 13:1 says, "Though I speak with the tongues of men and of angels, and have not charity, I am become *as* sounding brass, or a tinkling cymbal."
- **Enjoy the journey** and don't waste the beauty of the present by being overly goal oriented. It is important to plan ahead but don't miss out on the *now*. These *are* "the good old days!"

If you do these things every day, you will find yourself right in the middle of a full blown ministry. Perhaps a ministry title will come but titles are mere designations to things in which we specialize. Titles do not come easily but should represent proven ministries that are tested. Titles given too early can damage tender hearts if we are not careful. Don't seek a title before you have learned, submitted, become a faithful follower and have the endorsement of your direct *mentor*.

We start "ministry" with that which is directly in front of us. Our idea of the word "ministry" is often just a thing we do rather than the way we live. How can we effectively have a *ministry* if we don't know any sinners? What good is preaching in a pulpit if we don't **show** love to both believers and sinners? How can we influence the lost if we don't speak with them? When is the last time we ate with a sinner? Jesus did it.

Ministry is much more grass roots than we think. Earned titles in ministry should be a result of one going through the process of selflessness, learning, and submitting to the leadership that God has placed over us. No one should ever receive a title until they have gone through the ministry process of service to others. Even our political process could benefit from understanding the fundamentals of true ministry. Ministry is not for the purpose of building our egos or creating a constituency of people who love us. Its design is to lift up the name of Jesus for the Father's sake. Again, it is not about us at all.

Assignments extend to every believer. Because of this it cannot be about us. Ministry is about the purposes of God and is by nature, designed to accomplish His end goal. There is a story of a young minister who was fresh out of seminary that went to a church to volunteer to be a part of their ministry. As a volunteer he was there temporarily while his resumes were circulating among several vacancies in the area. The pastor called on him to sweep the floors preparing for a certain event they were having. The young man's face grimaced with a look of consternation. He said, "I'm an ordained minister of the Gospel with a Master's degree!" The wise older pastor smiled and simply said, "Welcome to ministry." Ministry should not be about status or self-worth. It's about Jesus' worth. We are nothing more than **servants** (Gk. "doulos" meaning slaves). Becoming arrogant about

1 service to the King is the **antithesis** of what Christianity is
2 all about. It is indeed a privilege to serve Him but arrogance
3 separates us from His presence. Clearly that is counter to our
4 original goal. Let us be humble before Him. He is God and
5 we are not. We need Him. He does **not** *need* us.
6
7   Our assignment is truly right in front of us. It begins
8 with a heart of love for others and obedience to the King.
9 True ministry occurs when we touch the lost that are in fact
10 desperate for that which only Christ can offer. If we believe
11 ministry is comprised of popularity and easy pay, we have a
12 hard lesson coming! If we can't find the kindness to open the
13 door for someone else, the likelihood of being willing to
14 suffer for rude and belligerent people is *nil*. If we don't see
15 the ministry in sweeping a floor, perhaps we have the wrong
16 idea about what real ministry is. If we can't put others before
17 us, we won't survive the difficulties of the role at all. In other
18 words, ministry is right in front of us. You may be a gifted
19 teacher but if you can't live the life that you teach about,
20 perhaps it is time to back up and punt. My dad had a saying
21 that he grew up hearing and using. When he saw something
22 poorly done he would say, "You need to go back and lick
23 your calf over." That was of course a farm phrase and every
24 farmer understands it but for those who may be city slickers,
25 it means if you don't do it right the first time, you need to go
26 back and do it again. Let's not get the cart before the horse
27 out of desperation for the need of workers in our churches.
28 Let's see what's right in front of us and start there. Start by
29 living for Jesus with your whole heart. Surrender to His
30 amazing character. Desire to be like Him. Seek His face
31 continually. If you'll take one step, He'll take two! Put into
32 practice the concept of putting others above you. That's a
33 great place to gain a simple understanding about
34 assignments. Once we do this, our purpose comes into focus.
35 It's powerful and it works!

Chapter 12
It's Right in Front of You

Key Study Words in Context

1. <u>Ministry</u> – (Pg. 125, #31), the act of service to others in the name of Jesus.

2. <u>Self-examination</u> – (Pg. 126, #1), an introspective survey, closely looking at one's own condition.

3. <u>Self-discipline</u> – (Pg. 126, #6), to maintain a personal set of rules by which to live, bringing one's self under control of a specific thought process.

4. <u>Deliberately</u> – (Pg. 127, #11), intentionally.

5. <u>Mentor</u> – (Pg. 127, #35), one who trains others, an intentional effort to lead someone in a specific way.

6. <u>Antithesis</u> – (Pg. 129, #1), the opposite, the example of wrong, converse.

7. <u>Nil</u> – (Pg. 129, #14), zero, nothing, of no affect.

Workbook Activity

1. What is wrong with only seeking titles to satisfy our need for assignments? (Pg. 125, #4-16)

2. Why is personal examination so critical to the success of an assignment? (Pg. 125, #18-35; Pg. 126, #1-3)

3. Discuss at length things that make working an assignment more meaningful.
   (Pg. 126, #5-33; Pg. 127, #1-35)

4. Ministry begins with a call from God. That means it isn't something that we only do; it is who we are. Explain this in detail. (Pg. 128, #1-8)

5. What is the true design of ministry? (Pg. 128, #10-20)

6. It is a privilege to receive an assignment from God. Why is it important to remember this in life?
   (Pg. 128, #22-36; Pg. 129, #1-5)

7. Loving others is at the core of every assignment. Discuss where this love comes from and how we should apply it in every event. (Pg. 129, #7-35)

Chapter 13
For the Win!

It would be foolish to think that anyone could ever succeed at anything without first believing that they can. In this quest to fulfill our purposes in life, we must accept the fact that the purpose is bigger than we are. At the end of our lives, how can we know we have accomplished our purpose, the very essence for our reason to be? As has been stated previously, we should live one event at a time with the knowledge that we are always on an assignment. That goes for the small events of the day all the way to the major problems that people face nearly *every day*. Tragedy always exposes what's underneath. But what if we had that which we need to go through the proverbial "hell or high water" experiences of life? What if we knew that our placement here on earth is not random and our purpose is to establish the light where there is darkness? Really, that one question encompasses the meaning behind our being here. Linger on that thought for a moment and deeply consider the truth that lies within that question. Are we a light to the world or do we add to the darkness?

Right now, the world sees little true faith. That is why they are able to abuse the Christian community so easily. We willfully gave up our influence or have sold it off to the world's highest bidder. We resist engaging in the fabric of society. Instead we recoil in fear without even so much as an audible whimper. How silly that is considering the amazing power that lives within these saved **jars of clay**. However, having extreme power and refusing to use it is the same as not having it at all. If we indeed have God's literal Spirit residing on the inside of these bodies and refuse to utilize it, then clearly we have missed something somewhere. Not only do we have an assignment but we have the tools with which to accomplish His plan with relative ease. After all, we don't have to do the hard work. The Holy Spirit within us does that. Since that is true, why don't we see the power of God manifested in our churches and in our daily lives? If we really are here to do the work of the Lord, how is it that we are spiritually anemic and devoid of purpose?

It is no surprise to the Christian community at large that we have lost our way. We have failed to prefer God over man. We easily assimilate into a broken world and offer no threat of any magnitude to its ***propensity*** to propagate its evil culture. Here are some questions to think about.

- How would we respond if God began stirring His people making them uncomfortable and dissatisfied with their distant acquaintance of Him?
- What would we do if He placed inside each one of us a deep abiding yearning to know Him more?
- What would we do if He allowed us to suffer in a way that we could see the need to rise to the call of the Most High?
- What if in the middle of the night, God began to give us dreams of His power poured out upon His people?
- What if the Muslims around the world learned of Jesus in their dreams and converted to Him as a result?
- What if the pastors stopped being people pleasers and started preaching the unadulterated Gospel the way the prophets and apostles preached it?
- What would happen if people began fasting, praying, studying His Word and worshiping Him every day **BEFORE** they came to church?
- What would it be like if we walked in the Spirit when we entered the department store or the gas station? How would our assignments look then? Wouldn't

For the Win!

they be crystal clear to us? If we did this, we would not doubt the Divine persuasion of the Lord. We would walk in His power and His purpose.

- If we walked in our Divine assignment, wouldn't we be fearless and bold concerning the Gospel and its proliferation to the masses?

Just to be clear, this kind of living does not remove us from the world but it does put us in the leadership role. This makes us **proactive** rather than **reactive** to everything around us. The result would be, when we walk in a room filled with an evil and worldly atmosphere; the demons would tremble because they know that WE KNOW who we are in Christ. When we walk in Him we can do exactly that which He has called us to do without fail!

God didn't send us to this planet to flounder and flop around. He sent us here to establishment the Kingdom of God. Part of that commission is to share the Good News that Jesus came and died for our sins. Another part of our reason to be here is simply to obey His wishes and fulfill the biblical mandates of loving one another. We still have families, we still shop for groceries and we still live our lives normally, but our purposes are no longer our own. We don't become flakes and freaks but we know why we are here and that alone offers extreme fulfillment. Just what does God really want with us anyway? He wants us to establish the Kingdom of God on earth as it is in Heaven. He's taking it all back and we are soldiers on assignment sent to do just that. It's not a done deal for now. We are in the middle of the war of wars! We don't need physical guns or modern weaponry to accomplish what He is asking of us. Our assignment is to reestablish a spiritual Kingdom by which its very nature automatically modifies the physical world with spiritual *attributes*. Did you catch that? When the spiritual Kingdom of God is in force, crime rates fall, abortions go down,

1 suicide goes down, murders go down and the longer this
2 spiritual culture is in place, the better the numbers get.
3
4   One of our biggest challenges we have is in our own
5 culture. We are in a world culture war but it's not really about
6 what humans prefer so much as it is about what God and
7 Satan prefer. Satan wants absolute anarchy and destruction.
8 He wants to **annihilate** the culture of God. This is why
9 professors from major liberal universities liken Christians to
10 that of Nazis. They call that which is good, evil over and over
11 until the masses believe it. It is a cultural battle but God will
12 have the last word and in the end, He wins!
13
14   When we follow His orders, we are not responsible
15 for the outcome. We can't see the forest for the trees so it is
16 impossible for us to do the maneuvering and controlling of
17 the troops. We simply do as told and leave the results to God.
18 That way, we cannot take credit for the successes since that
19 all belongs to God anyway. If your assignment at the moment
20 is smiling and being kind to someone, don't underestimate
21 its value. It might be exactly what they need for the moment
22 assuring them that God is working behind the scene. Don't
23 be discouraged because you did not feed ten-thousand
24 hungry children this morning but you just may have
25 encouraged one who will. Few people today can recall the
26 name of the pastor, Mordecai Ham, who won Billy Graham
27 to faith in Christ. That does not negate the fact that although
28 this man is still unknown by most of us, he was nevertheless
29 used by God mightily for a purpose beyond his scope. He
30 will always be on record as winning *at least* one more to
31 Christ than Billy Graham! He could not have known the
32 outcome of his simple obedience but God did. Do you know
33 the name of the one who brought the evangelist Reinhardt
34 Bonnke to Jesus? Neither do I but God does. We may serve
35 in obscurity by human terms but not by God's view. No
36 servant of the Lord is obscure from His perspective and that

1 is the only point of view that truly matters. We do not have a
2 clue at the meaning or depth of our purpose but God sends
3 us on missions with His goals in mind. We do not need to
4 know why. We simply need to obey and trust Him for the big
5 picture. He will never ask us to do anything immoral or
6 anything that would oppose His Word. Once we understand
7 these rules of the game, we can function with peace and the
8 satisfaction of knowing that His plan is always best. That is
9 how we fulfill our purpose in life.
10
11 • We listen to Him through His Word and His Holy
12   Spirit.
13 • We give over to His **sovereign** will above all else.
14 • We walk with the expectation that He is always
15   looking after our best interests. "And we know that
16   all things work together for good to them that love
17   God, to them who are the called according to his
18   purpose." (Romans 8:28).
19 • We deliberately recognize the moment by moment
20   assignments.
21 • We know that our assignment is not just one big
22   thing; it's a culmination of many assignments.
23 • We stop looking at life's experiences as tests but
24   rather see them as ASSIGNMENTS with an intended
25   goal. Read that again! God does not need to test us
26   for His sake. He already knows us. He assigns us!
27
28   It is imperative that we not be enamored with the idea
29 that there is some utopic destination awaiting us if we only
30 align with the stars and stand on one foot, looking northward.
31 We have so wasted the good part of the journey by staring
32 intently at the possible end result that we have missed the
33 obvious. Slow down and notice what is in front of you. Look
34 into the eyes of those you love and breathe the fresh air of
35 purpose and intention. Say the words you think you would
36 regret not saying should you leave this world today. Hold on

to memories that bring you joy. Be proactive about making memories that are lasting. **Great memories are deliberately made; they don't just happen.** Give up bad memories that stifle and undermine God's purposes in your life.

Let me reiterate that it is essential that we cease from seeing every situation in life as a test and start seeing them as assignments. When people say that God is testing them, I wonder if they realize that God has no particular need to test us as though He doesn't already know how we think. That is a human perspective of God's motivation. Since He already knows what makes us tick and our physiology, His purposes must be different than many believe. If we do find ourselves in a dilemma, it serves as a mirror to us rather than a source to inform God of our current status. He knows. If we understand that He is sovereign, then we must conclude that our challenges and difficulties serve at least two distinct purposes.

1. He wants **us** to know what's inside of us since hardship reveals our true identities. He wants us to recognize our own need for growth. So things that come along that challenge us may solely be for the purpose of revealing to us our own short comings. This is useful for us to know where we need to grow and in what areas we are weakest. Remember that we are soldiers preparing for a wide variety of assignments.
2. He sent us into difficulty with our assignments to bring the Glory of God into that respective situation. Darkness is in the world but He sent us here to bring light. We bring light in suffering, pain, bad situations, loss, grief, divorce and every challenging circumstance. We must also remember to bring glory to Him in good times!

For the Win!

I believe both of these concepts are plausible and meaningful. The simple fact that we are here in an evil world is a strong indicator that we have a reason and a purpose to be here. Our assignment is to be salt and light. Since that is true, let it begin with the simplest of actions. If we get this basic fact, we will find the peace for which we have searched a lifetime. Seek to be in the center of His will. Don't fight it by kicking and screaming each time a new assignment arises. Accept it and bring His Glory into the scene. He will reward you over and over.

These are exciting days! The fact that God has not abandoned us and left us to our own demise is exciting and exhilarating. God *is* our refuge and our strength! Jesus said, Apart from me, you can do nothing. His Word also states in Philippians 4:13 that "I can do all things through Christ which strengthens me..." Let us take on the idea that our assignments are Divinely inspired and we are here for His purposes. He sent us here to reclaim planet earth for His Kingdom. We won't do it with guns and ammo. We will do it through prayer and obedience to His Word. This is the most exciting time in the history of our planet. I believe that every single day we have an assignment awaiting our attention. Let's do it for Jesus! Only that which we do for Christ will last. There is nothing more fulfilling or more completing than serving the Lord well, starting with the little things. Deliberately live this way and experience the refreshing of being in the center of God's will. Nothing compares to that, nothing at all. Living this way is the most meaningful and peaceful existence on the planet. It's always all about Him. If we will only surrender, we will know peace in the truest sense of the word.

Now go, be about the Father's business. Remember that you are always on an assignment and never underestimate the value of it, no matter the size. God knows

1   what it's all about and that's really all that matters. We are
2   here for a short time. Let us determine that we will use our
3   time wisely, effectively and meaningfully. Heaven awaits us
4   and it will exponentially exceed all of our expectations. It
5   will be worth every effort. Until then, push the Kingdom of
6   God and the plan of Salvation. Love deliberately and pour
7   into everyone you meet. It could be something as simple as
8   a smile. If that's what God orders then do it. If he wants you
9   to bring groceries to a neighbor, then do it. Listen intently,
10 follow His Word and live out your assignment with fervor.
11 The joy of the Lord will be yours! This changes everything
12 and makes life full and rich and certainly worth living! Now
13 go! Your mission field awaits!

Chapter 13
For the Win!

Key Study Words in Context

1. <u>Jars of Clay</u> – (Pg. 133, #30), human bodies formed from the earth.

2. <u>Propensity</u> – (Pg. 134, #12), a natural and possibly intense inclination.

3. <u>Attributes</u> (verb) – (Pg. 135, #35), something that adds to, expressed as gifts of character or personality.

4. <u>Annihilate</u> – (Pg. 136, #8), to utterly destroy, to completely eliminate, to overwhelm.

5. <u>Sovereign</u> – (Pg. 137, #13), supreme power or authority, stands on its own merit, independent of other powers, vastly superior above all others to the point of extreme advantage and independence.

Workbook Activities

1. How does tragedy expose what lies beneath the surface? (Pg. 133, #4-22)

2. Why is it that most Christians today do not have any idea of what their assignment is?
(Pg. 133, #24-34; Pg. 134, #1-7)

3. Discuss the questions explaining what might happen if we preferred God's ways over man's ways. Please carefully ponder each question listed.
(Pg.134, #9-36; Pg. 135, #1-6)

4. What is the advantage to being proactive as opposed to reactive? (Pg. 135, # 8-15)

5. Why are we here? What does God really want with us? (Pg. 135, #17-36; Pg. 136, #1-2)

6. Why is culture an issue? How does it change our world? (Pg. 136, #4-12)

For the Win!

7. Explain why we don't always need to know the reason why God asks us to do a simple assignment. What can happen if we obey? (Pg. 136, #14-36; Pg. 137, #1-9)

8. Discuss some of the rules of the game. (Pg. 137, #11-26)

9. What advantage do we have by slowing down and taking notice of the gifts of God in life? How does this help us grasp the beauty of the journey?
(Pg. 137, #28-36; Pg. 138, #1-4)

10. Why is it essential that we see life as an assignment rather than a constant test? (Pg. 138, #6-18)

11. Explain at least two distinct purposes for our assignment. (Pg. 138, #20-35)

For the Win!

12. The world needs us to be here. Why is that? (Pg. 139, #1-10)

13. Approaching our assignments from the right perspective is imperative. Discuss why this is. (Pg. 139, #12-32)

14. Explain how loving deliberately plays into our assignments. (Pg. 139, #34-36; Pg. 140, #1-13)

15. Discuss how this study has helped you. Has it changed the way you see your assignments?

And they overcame him
by the blood of the Lamb,
and by the word of
their testimony;
and they did not love their
lives to the death.

Revelation 12:11

Please contact Dr. Devon Blanton at:

Research Triangle Park Community Church
P.O. Box 11236
Durham, NC 27703

For bookings, please contact:
Tina Owen, Executive Assistant
919-596-4352 (Church office)
Email: tinaowenrtpcc@gmail.com